compassionate knitting

compassionate knitting

FINDING BASIC GOODNESS IN THE WORK OF OUR HANDS

Tara Jon Manning

TUTTLE PUBLISHING

Tokyo • Rutland, Vermont • Singapore

First published in 2006 by Tuttle Publishing, an imprint of Periplus Editions (HK) Ltd., with editorial offices at 364 Innovation Drive, North Clarendon, Vermont 05759.

Library of Congress Cataloging-in-Publication Data

Manning, Tara Jon, 1968–
 Compassionate knitting : finding basic goodness in the work of our hands / Tara Jon Manning.
  p. cm. Includes index.
  ISBN-13: 978-0-8048-3707-1 (pbk.)
  ISBN-10: 0-8048-3707-4 (pbk.)
 1. Knitting—Patterns. 2. Handicraft—Religious aspects—Buddhism. I. Title.
TT820.M12 2006
746.43'2041—dc22
2005019731

Distributed by

NORTH AMERICA,
LATIN AMERICA & EUROPE
Tuttle Publishing
364 Innovation Drive
North Clarendon, VT 05759-9436
Tel: (802) 773-8930
Fax: (802) 773-6993
info@tuttlepublishing.com
www.tuttlepublishing.com

JAPAN
Tuttle Publishing
Yaekari Building, 3rd Floor
5-4-12 Ōsaki
Shinagawa-ku
Tokyo 141 0032
Tel: (03) 5437-0171
Fax: (03) 5437-0755
tuttle-sales@gol.com

ASIA PACIFIC
Berkeley Books Pte. Ltd.
130 Joo Seng Road
#06-01/03 Olivine Building
Singapore 368357
Tel: (65) 6280-1330
Fax: (65) 6280-6290
inquiries@periplus.com.sg
www.periplus com

First edition
09 08 07 06   10 9 8 7 6 5 4 3 2

Photography by Bill Manning • Photo styling by Tara Jon Manning
Technical edits by Lori Gayle • Design by Gopa & Ted2, Inc.

Printed in Canada

TUTTLE PUBLISHING ® is a registered trademark of Tuttle Publishing, a division of Periplus Editions (HK) Ltd.

For Molly and Sammy

thanks

Bill, Jack and Zane, Jennifer Brown, Lori Gayle, Barbara Lavender, Jamie Little, Tuttle Publishing, Linda Roghaar, Margaret Klein Wilson, Mindful Knitters everywhere.

contents

part three: knitter

preface

mindful knitter, compassionate knitter

IN *Mindful Knitting,* the curious knitter was invited to explore the subtleties of mindfulness while knitting. By learning a simple technique of mindfulness meditation, and applying the basic tenet of this technique to the work of their hands, *Mindful Knitting* asked knitters to view their craft as a method of meditation and a means to generate compassion. Viewing our craft in this way we see how it can act as a source of benefit to ourselves and to the world at large. When we knit mindfully—bringing our attention to the work at hand—we are able to see things a little more clearly, slow the world down just a little bit, and allow ourselves to be just a little more gentle toward ourselves and others. As a result, we begin to see our place in our own lives a little more clearly, and see how we can be of benefit to others. This basic root of compassion just seems to spill out of us.

This leads us to the next step—compassionate knitting. We can choose to use our "mindful knitting" as a means of contributing positive thought and calm to a simple situation in our own lives or to a situation greater than ourselves. And, what better vehicle to express this out-flowing of compassion than knitting—where the things we create can literally act as a metaphor for giving, warmth, hope, and appreciation of the everyday.

Compassionate Knitting puts the insightful knitter in touch with the magic of the world and each individual, and shows us the innate capacity for compassion within each of us. The practice of mindfulness is one in which we are constantly taking the first steps on that trembling and exciting ground of open, contemplative awareness. Compassionate knitters are invited to explore the notion known as the basic goodness in all things. When we allow ourselves to be fully present, we experience this essence and power of basic goodness—the ever-present potential within all beings to wake up.

heaven, earth, and knitter

The compassionate knitter's journey is one in which we join heaven and earth. The notion heaven, earth, and man (or in our case, knitter), is one of a world—and a state of being—where a beautiful sense of balance and unity exist. Heaven offers open sky, and the essence of sacredness and inspiration. Earth is fertile ground—it is receptive and solid. As we experience the purity of heaven and earth, we "join" them—allowing through our direct experience of each unique moment the existence of a simple and primordial way of simply being.

The experience of joining heaven and earth is very powerful, yet usually lost on us as we go about our busy days and habitual patterns of living. However, by reminding ourselves to be aware of this natural occurrence—one that takes place simply because we are there—each of us can see the potential for magic the world has to offer. In being aware of your place as the catalyst that joins heaven and earth, you unleash a natural sense of confidence and innate, unstoppable capacity for compassion. There is a natural harmony offered by this view of the world, and an invitation to connect to the vivid nature of our experience. In this place, we see magic everywhere, we open our peripheral vision to see the wide-open sky, and the possibility to live fully in that and every moment. Taking our place in this order allows us to view our experience and our world as magical and sacred. Joining heaven and earth becomes a type of mindfulness practice, bringing us to rest on the spot.

So, in joining heaven and earth we unleash a sense of natural confidence and trust in ourselves. By resting in an experience, in a moment, in a sensation we naturally move outside of ourselves. This is the basis of our innate sense of compassion. As we let go of our own drama and thoughts of ourselves, we instinctually become sensitive to others. Cultivating this instinct brings us to a place of acknowledging the basic goodness in all things and allows us to become more available to others without agenda.

the compassionate knitting project collection

This collection of patterns expands on the theme of *Mindful Knitting*, yet introduces new readers to the notion of purposefully developing a fascination for and relationship with contemplative experience that can be found on the needles. Twenty projects—ranging from small, easy-to-knit gifts to elaborate, exquisite Asian inspired pieces— offer a sense of personal ritual in their creation, use, or presentation. Some projects present contemplative themes while others will play with notions of the magical and mindful. These projects will invite the knitter into a deeper relationship with what is at hand—the actual project, its purpose, its recipient, its theme, how it invokes a mindful knitting moment. *Compassionate Knitting* offers a footpath and guidance for this continuous and exciting journey.

All of the projects presented here are inspired by elements of the inner and outer experiences of the world and the harmony of heaven, earth, and knitter. Some pieces were found during a moment of contemplative inspiration during a walk in the woods—experiencing the integration of heaven earth and man—and seeing very acutely through the eyes of nowness. The gloriousness of a moment is translated into items to be crafted by hands and items that remind us to stay aware of that sense of magic. Other projects were inspired by the joy of my children, the great honor I feel to know them and the constant reminder that they are a gift from heaven. Still other pieces were the product of the desire to reach out to others, to invite a moment of basic goodness or delight into someone's day with a reminder that they are special to me.

All these points of inspiration lead back to a place within each knitter that drives us to knit—to create. Be it on a walk through the woods, in mediation, or mindful knitting, each knitter finds their place of magic as we each join the components of the universe through the work of our hands. There we explore our own basic goodness and expression of compassion without complication. As we knit to soothe, to offer comfort, to offer ourselves a break from the rest of our day, we find a gift. In our knitting we explore elements of ourselves, elements of the natural world, elements of giving and receiving. Use these projects to explore your own innate compassion, to learn new skills, to practice mindful knitting or simply to knit. May you enjoy your continuing knitting journey, and may the work of your hands be of benefit.

part one

HEAVEN

Open sky, limitlessness, and boundless inspiration.

CLOUD PILLOW

Clouds can provide us with much inspiration. Not only do they evoke the vastness and beauty of the sky but they can remind us of serene moments spent letting our minds wander or grand moments of creativity as we watch mythic creatures roll by. This pillow reminds us to keep our heads in the clouds—to find our truth there; to dream.

Knit in a luxuriously soft hand-dyed alpaca blend, this beautiful pillow cover features a stylized oriental cloud motif with embroidered embellishment on the front, and a classic Chinese chintz-inspired stripe on the back. Knit in one piece and seamed at the sides, this fanciful project fits a standard 16" (40-cm) square knife-edge pillow form available at craft stores.

FINISHED SIZE: About 16" (40.5 cm) square.

YARN: Blue Sky Alpacas Worsted Hand Dyes (50% alpaca, 50% wool; 100 yards [91 meters]/100 grams): 2 skeins main color (MC); 1 skein each of two contrast colors (CC1 and CC2). Shown in #2007 Light Blue (MC), #2003 Ecru (CC1), and #2001 Dark Blue (CC2).

NEEDLES: US 9 (5.5 mm), or size to give gauge.

NOTIONS: Measuring tape, yarn needle, scissors, stitch markers, 16" (40-cm) square knife-edge pillow form.

GAUGE: 16 sts and 23 rows = 4" (10 cm) in St St.

STITCHES USED:
Stockinette Stitch (St St): Knit all sts on RS rows, and purl all sts on WS rows.

▲ *See page 97*

15

Seed Stitch (worked over an odd number of sts)
All rows: *K1, p1; rep from * to last st, end k1.

NOTE: Cloud motifs from chart are worked in St St intarsia technique. Use a separate ball or butterfly of yarn for each color, and twist yarns at the color changes to avoid leaving holes.

Instructions

Front: With dark blue, CO 65 sts. Work in Seed St for 8 rows, ending with a WS row. On the next row (RS), knit across all sts. Change to light blue and purl 1 WS row. Work Rows 9–12 of Checkered Pattern chart once (do not work stripe Rows 1–8). Change to light blue and work even in St St until piece measures about 1½" (3.8 cm) from top of checkered patt, or about 4" (10 cm) from CO edge, ending with a WS row.

Clouds: Set position of first cloud motif as foll: (RS) K24 with light blue, place marker (pm, optional), work Row 1 of Cloud chart over next 16 sts, pm, K25 with light blue. Slipping markers every row (sl m), cont in St St, working 16 marked sts according to Cloud chart until Row 22 of chart has been completed. Work 6 rows even in St St with light blue only, ending with a WS row. Set position of second cloud as foll: K6 with light blue, place marker (pm, optional), work Row 1 of Cloud chart over next 16 sts, pm, k43 with light blue. Cont in St St, working 16 marked sts according to Cloud chart until Row 14 of chart has been completed. On the next row (RS; Row 15 of second cloud motif), set position of third cloud as foll: K6 with light blue, sl m, work Row 15 of Cloud chart over next 16 sts, sl m, k14 with light blue, pm, work Row 1 of Cloud chart over next 16 sts, pm, k13 with light blue. Work even in established patts until Row 22 of second cloud (Row 8 of third cloud) has been completed. Remove markers for second cloud as you come to them. Working 16 rem marked sts for third cloud as established, and work all other sts in light blue work until Row 22 of third cloud has been completed. Work even until piece meas 15¾" (40 cm) from CO edge, ending with a RS row. Knit 1 WS row to form turning ridge along top edge of pillow.

Back: Change to Checkered Pattern chart, and rep Rows 1–12 six times, then work

Rows 1–8 once more—80 rows completed for pillow back; piece meas about 14" (35.5 cm) from turning ridge. With dark blue, knit 1 RS row, then work in Seed St for 8 rows. BO all sts loosely in Seed St.

Embroidery: With dark blue and yarn needle, embroider outline and center swirl on each cloud using backstitch. Secure ends. (See Emroidery Technique on page 25.)

Finishing: Sew side seams. Weave in ends. Insert pillow form into bottom opening and invisibly sew bottom of pillow closed. Rest your head and enjoy your dreams.

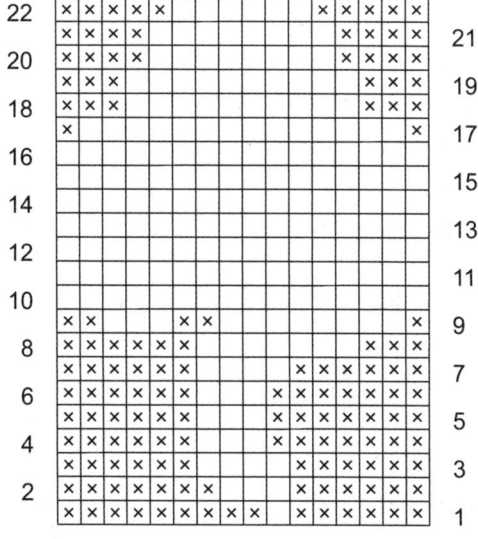

▲ *Cloud Pattern Chart*

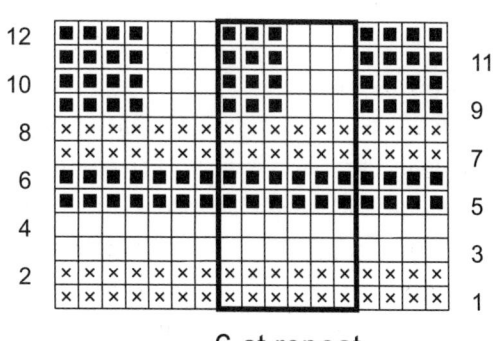

6-st repeat

▲ *Checkered Pattern Chart*

| × | Light Blue: knit on RS, purl on WS |
| Ecru: knit on RS, purl on WS |
| ■ | Dark Blue: knit on RS, purl on WS |

Heaven and Stars Baby Set

Inspired by the beauty and wonder of the night skies, this outfit is the perfect reminder that your baby is a little gift from heaven. This set of quick-to-knit overalls with matching cardigan in easy-care cotton or cotton blend yarn features intarsia stars in yellow that twinkle on a midnight blue background. Embroidered hints of stardust and tails of shooting stars make this a heavenly scene.

Cardigan

Finished Size: To fit 6–12 months (18–24 months); shown in size 18–24 months
Chest measurement: 25 (28)";
(63.5 [71] cm)
Total length: 10½ (12)"; (26.5 [30.5] cm)
Sleeve length: 8 (9)"; (20.5 [23] cm)

Yarn: Brown Sheep Company Cotton Fleece (80% cotton, 20% wool; 215 yards [197 meters]/100 grams): 2 (2) skeins main color (MC); 1 (1) skein contrast color (CC). Shown in #CW590 Lapis (MC) and #CW620 Banana (CC).
Note: One skein of CC is enough to make both the cardigan and overalls in this set.

Needles: US 6 (4 mm), or size to give gauge.

▲ *See page 97*

NOTIONS: Five ⅝" (1.6 cm) buttons, measuring tape, yarn needle, scissors, stitch holders, crochet hook size G/6 (4 mm), crochet hook size J/10 (6 mm), stitch markers (optional). Buttons shown: Little Stars glass buttons from Moving Mud.

GAUGE: 20 sts and 28 rows = 4" (10 cm) in St St. Check your gauge before you begin.

STITCHES USED:
Stockinette Stitch (St St): Knit all sts on RS rows, and purl all sts on WS rows.

TECHNIQUES USED:
Two-Row, Two-Stitch Buttonhole
Row 1: (RS) Work to position indicated in directions, BO 2 sts, work to end.
Row 2: (WS) Work to gap created by binding off 2 sts in the previous row, CO 2 sts over the gap, work to end.

Three-Needle Bind-Off Technique
Place sts to be joined on two needles so that the right sides of the fabric face each other and the tips of both needles point in the same direction. Hold the two needles parallel to each other in your left hand to act as a single LH needle. Using a third needle as the RH needle, insert this RH needle through the first st on the front LH needle and then through the first st on the back LH needle. Knit the two sts together as one and slide them both off their respective needles. Repeat once more—2 sts on RH needle. Pass the first st over the second to BO 1 st. Repeat the process until all sts are bound off. Cut yarn, leaving a 6"–10" (15–25 cm) tail and draw the tail through the last st to finish.

Instructions

Back: Loosely CO 62 (70) sts with MC. Work in St St, working small, medium, and large

a note on buttonholes

For a woman's or girl's sweater, make buttonholes on right front and sew buttons to left front. For a man's or boy's sweater, make buttonholes on left front and sew buttons to right front. (Also see Intuitive Knitting Tip: Buttonhole Placement on page 93.)

intarsia star motifs in CC according to the charts on page 25, placing them according to the drawings on page 18 or as desired. Work even until piece meas 5½ (6½") (14 [16.5] cm) from CO, ending with a WS row.

Armhole shaping: BO 2 sts at beg of next 2 rows—58 (66) sts. Cont in patt from chart until piece meas 10¼ (11¾)" (26 [30] cm) from CO, ending with a WS row.

Back neck shaping: Work across 15 (19) sts, BO center 28 sts, work 15 (19) sts—piece meas about 10½ (12)" (26.5 [30.5] cm) from CO. Place shoulder sts on separate stitch holders.

Left front: Loosely CO 34 (38) sts with MC. Work in St St, working small, medium, and large intarsia star motifs in CC according to chart or as desired. Work even until piece meas 5½ (6½") (14 [16.5] cm) from CO, ending with a WS row.

Armhole shaping: BO 2 sts at beg of next RS row—32 (36) sts. Cont in patt from chart until piece meas 8½ (10)" (21.5 [25.5] cm) from CO, ending with a RS row.

Neck shaping: BO 12 sts at beg of next WS row—20 (24) sts. Dec 1 st at neck edge every RS row 5 times—15 (19) sts. Cont in patt

from chart until piece meas 10½ (12)" (26.5 [30.5] cm) from CO, or same length as back. Place shoulder sts on holder.

Right front: Work as for left front, reversing shaping by binding off for armhole at beg of a WS row and binding off for neck at beg of a RS row, and at the same time, make five two-row, two-stitch buttonholes at center front edge, the lowest ½" (1.3 cm) up from CO, and the rest about 1¾ (2¼)" (4.5 [5.5] cm) apart, with the highest buttonhole about ½" (1.3 cm) below beg of neck shaping as foll: (RS) Work 2 sts, BO 2 sts for buttonhole, work to end; complete buttonhole in next row by CO 2 sts over gap in previous row. Place shoulder sts on holder.

Shoulder joining: Using three-needle bind-off technique, join shoulders together, right sides facing, carefully matching left front to left back and right front to right back, making sure that the front piece with the buttonholes is the right front. The side of the garment with the three-needle bind-off ridge is the WS of the garment.

Sleeves: The sleeves are worked from the armhole down to the cuff. In order to make the star motifs appear right side up when the cardigan is worn, turn the charts upside down and work each star from its top down to its base as you work the sleeves. With RS facing and MC, using smaller crochet hook to assist if desired, pick up 54 (60) sts evenly between armhole notches, with first st picked up at base of notch (notches will be sewn into place later). Work in St St, working small, medium, and large intarsia star motifs in CC according to chart or as desired. At the same time, shape sleeves by dec 1 st each end of needle every 3 rows 10 times—34 (40) sts. Work even until sleeve meas 8 (9)" (20.5 [23] cm) from shoulder pickup. Loosely BO all sts.

Make a second sleeve the same as the first.

Finishing: Sew sleeve extensions in place at underarm notch. Sew sleeve and side seams. Weave in the ends. Steam block lightly if needed.

With CC (or MC if you prefer) and larger crochet hook, work a row of single crochet all around the lower edge, front opening, and neck opening. Work a row of single crochet around each sleeve cuff.

Securely sew 5 buttons to left front corresponding with buttonhole positions.

Embellishment: Using CC threaded on a tapestry needle, embroider tiny stars, French knots, and backstitch swirls. (See Embroidery Techniques on page 25.) Secure all ends.

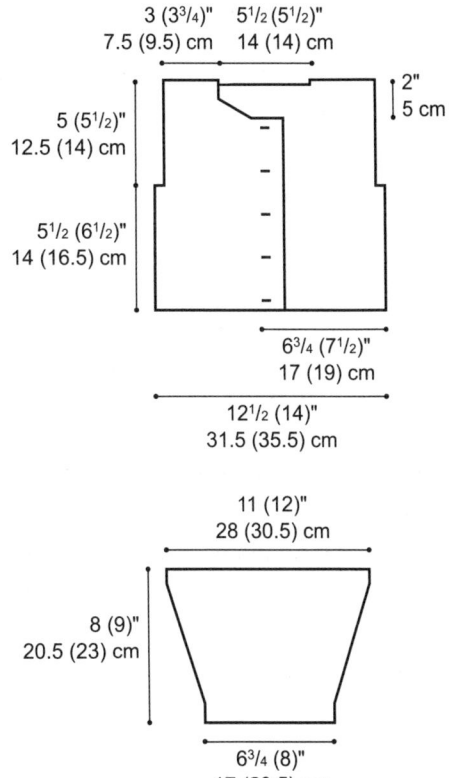

▲ *Heaven and Stars Cardigan*

Overalls

Finished Size: To fit 6–12 months (12–18 months, 18–24 months); shown in size 18–24 months
Chest measurement: 25 (26½, 28)"; (63.5 [67.5, 71] cm)
Length from lower edge to armhole: 14¾ (15¾, 16¾)"; (37.5 [40, 42.5] cm)
Armhole height to end of straps: 6¼ (6¾, 7¼)"; (16 [17, 18.5] cm)

Yarn: Brown Sheep Company Cotton Fleece (80% cotton, 20% wool; 215 yards [197 meters]/100 grams): 2 (3, 3) skeins main color (MC); 1 (1, 1) skein contrast color (CC). Shown in #CW590 Lapis (MC) and #CW620 Banana (CC).
Note: One skein of CC is enough to make both the cardigan and overalls in this set.

Needles: US 4 (3.5 cm) and US 6 (4 mm), or size to give gauge.

Notions: Seven ⅝" (1.6 cm) buttons (five for legs and two for

◀ *See page 97*

shoulder straps), measuring tape, yarn needle, scissors, stitch holders, crochet hook size G/6 (4 mm), crochet hook size J/10 (6 mm). Shoulder straps buttons shown: Little Stars glass buttons from Moving Mud.

Gauge: 20 sts and 28 rows = 4" (10 cm) in St St. Check your gauge before you begin.

Stitches Used:
Stockinette Stitch (St St): Knit all sts on RS rows, and purl all sts on WS rows.

Knit 1, Purl 1 Rib (worked over an even number of sts):
All rows: *K1, p1; rep from * to end.

Techniques Used:
Two-Row, Two-Stitch Buttonhole, Three-Needle Bind-Off Technique (see page 19 for both).

Instructions
Note: The front and back are identical except for the buttonholes at the top of the front straps.

Front legs: With MC and larger needles,

loosely cast on 28 (30, 32) sts. Work in St St beg with a RS row, working small, medium, and large intarsia star motifs in CC according to the charts on page 25, placing them according to the drawings on page 18 or so desired. At the same time, inc 1 st each end of needle every 6 (6, 8) rows 5 times—38 (40, 42) sts. Work even until leg meas 5 (5½, 6)" (12.5 [14, 15] cm) from CO, ending with a WS row. Place sts on holder.

Make a second leg the same as the first, leaving sts on needle.

Front lower body: With RS facing, work across 38 (40, 42) sts of leg on needle, CO 2 sts, return 38 (40, 42) sts held sts of first leg to needle, and with same ball of yarn work across sts of first leg—78 (82, 86) sts. Work even, cont to place star motifs as desired until piece meas 9 (10, 11)" (23 [25.5, 28] cm) from CO for legs, or 4 (4½, 5)" (10 [11.5, 12.5] cm) above joining row, ending with a WS row. Beg with the next RS row, dec 1 st each end of needle every 5 rows 8 times, ending with a WS row—62 (66, 70) sts; piece measures about 14¾ (15¾, 16¾)" (37.5 [40, 42.5] cm) from CO for legs.

Shape armholes: BO 6 sts at the beginning of next 2 rows—50 (54, 58) sts. Then dec 1 st each end of needle every other row 8 times, ending with a WS row—34 (38, 42) sts; armholes meas about 2½" (6.5 cm). Work even until armhole meas 2¾ (3¼, 3¾)" (7 [8.5, 9.5] cm), or 17½ (19, 20½)" (44.5 [48.5, 52] cm) from CO for legs, ending with a WS row.

Shape neck: Work 11 (13, 13) sts, join second ball of yarn, BO center 12 (12, 16) sts, work to end—11 (13, 13) sts at each side. Working each side separately, dec 1 st at neck each edge every other row 3 times—8 (10, 10) sts at each side.

Shoulder straps: Work even on remaining 8 (10, 10) sts at each side until armholes meas 5¾ (6¼, 6¾)" (14.5 [16, 17] cm) from armhole bind off, ending with a WS row. Beginning with the next row, make a two-row two-stitch buttonhole positioned in the center of each strap as follows: (RS) Work 3 (4, 4) sts, BO 2 sts for buttonhole, work 3 (4, 4) sts to end; complete buttonhole in next row by CO 2 sts over gap in previous row. Work even until straps meas 6¼ (6¾, 7¼)" (16 [17, 18.5] cm) from beg of armhole, and piece meas 21 (22½, 24)" (53.5 [57, 61] cm) total from leg CO. BO all sts.

Back: Work same as front to beg of shoulder strap instructions—8 (10, 10) sts at each side.

Work even, omitting buttonholes, until straps meas 6¼ (6¾, 7¼)" (16 [17, 18.5] cm) from beg of armhole. BO all sts.

Front inseam buttonhole band: Sew front to back at sides from CO edge to armhole shaping. Mark positions for 5 buttonholes along front leg opening, with 1 buttonhole ½" (1.3 cm) up from CO edge of each leg, and rem 3 buttonholes evenly spaced in between; middle buttonhole should be centered on 2 sts CO for leg join. With RS facing, smaller needles and MC, using smaller crochet hook to assist if desired, pick up 28 (30, 32) sts along inside right front leg from CO edge to leg join, pick up 2 sts from sts CO for join, then pick up 28 (30, 32) sts along inside left front leg to CO edge—58 (62, 66) sts. Work in knit 1, purl 1 rib for 2 rows. On the next 2 rows, make five two-row, two-stitch buttonholes at marked positions. Work even in rib for 3 more rows—buttonhole band meas about 1" (2.5 cm) from pick up. BO all sts in rib.

Back inseam button band: With RS facing, smaller needles and MC, using smaller crochet hook to assist if desired, pick up 28 (30, 32) sts along inside left back leg from CO edge to leg join, pick up 2 sts from sts CO for join, then pick up 28 (30, 32) sts along inside right back leg to CO edge—58 (62, 66) sts.

Work in knit 1, purl 1 rib for 7 rows—buttonhole band meas about 1" (2.5 cm) from pick up. BO all sts in rib.

Finishing: Weave in the ends. Steam block lightly if needed.

With CC (or MC if you prefer) and larger crochet hook, work a row of single crochet all around the top opening as foll: *Work up one armhole, across top of strap, around neck opening, across top of next strap, and down to beg of armhole; rep from * for the other side.

Securely sew 5 buttons to back inseam band corresponding with buttonhole positions on front inseam band, and sew 1 button to top of each back strap corresponding to buttonhole on front strap.

Embellishment: Using CC threaded on a tapestry needle, embroider tiny stars, French knots, and backstitch swirls as suggested in the drawings on page 18 and in the detail to the right. Secure all ends.

Detail of Heaven and ▶
Stars embroidery

Emboidery Techniques

 *Beginning French Knot*

 Finished French Knot

 *Lazy Daisy*

 *Backstitch*

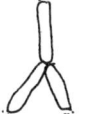 *Tiny Star Step One (use backstitch)*

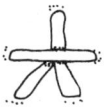 *Tiny Star Step One (use backstitch)*

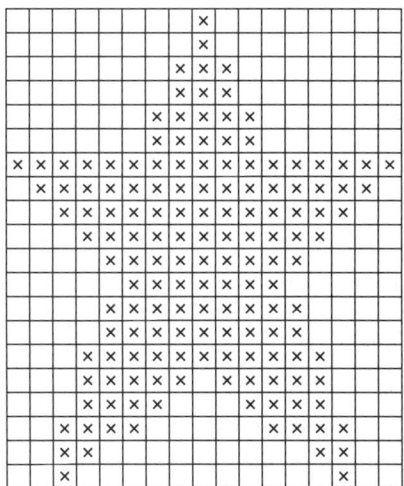

▲ *Large Star, 17 sts and 20 rows*

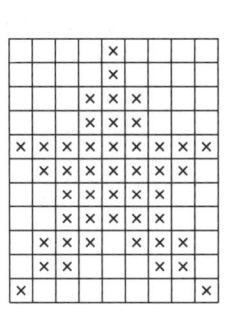

◄ *Medium Star, 9 sts and 11 rows*

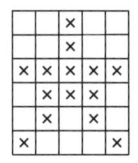

◄ *Small Star, 5 sts and 6 rows*

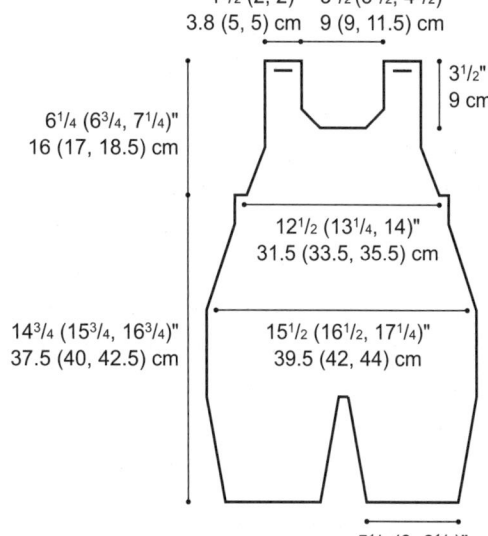

1¹/₂ (2, 2)"   3¹/₂ (3¹/₂, 4¹/₂)"
3.8 (5, 5) cm   9 (9, 11.5) cm

3¹/₂"
9 cm

6¹/₄ (6³/₄, 7¹/₄)"
16 (17, 18.5) cm

12¹/₂ (13¹/₄, 14)"
31.5 (33.5, 35.5) cm

14³/₄ (15³/₄, 16³/₄)"
37.5 (40, 42.5) cm

15¹/₂ (16¹/₂, 17¹/₄)"
39.5 (42, 44) cm

▲ *Heaven and Stars Overalls*   5¹/₂ (6, 6¹/₂)"
14 (15, 16.5) cm

☐ MC: knit on RS, purl on WS

☒ CC: knit on RS, purl on WS

Autumn Leaves Blanket

This warm wrap or blanket in earth tones presents a scatter of felt leaves resting as if the cool fall breeze placed them there. Used as a wrap, it takes away the chill from a fall afternoon walk. Used as a blanket, it provides a cuddle of warmth in the early morning or while watching a favorite movie. This project has a focus on seasonal and elemental change. With its breezy poetic quality, physical movement of air and leaves of natural wool in stylized Japanese form, it reminds us of the gentle tremble of rustling leaves.

FINISHED SIZE: About 30" (76 cm) wide and 56" (142 cm) long.

YARN: Crystal Palace Iceland (100% wool; 109 yards [100 meters]/100 grams): 8 skeins. Shown in #3343 Tree Bark.

NEEDLES: US 13 (9 mm) 24" (60-cm) or longer circular (circ) needle, or size to give gauge.

◀ *See page 98*

NOTIONS: Measuring tape, yarn needle, scissors, crochet hook size J/10 (6 mm); 3 to 5 sheets of purchased burgundy/red-colored wool felt (or make your own, see About felt on page 27), scraps of wool yarn in autumn colors to embellish leaves, sharp-pointed hand sewing needle and sewing thread to match leaf color.

GAUGE: 12 sts and 15 rows = 4" (10 cm) in St St.

STITCHES USED:
Stockinette Stitch (St St): Knit all sts on RS rows, and purl all sts on WS rows.

NOTE: The sample shown has handmade felt leaves and Manos del Uruguay yarns for embellishment (100% wool; 137 yards [125 meters]/100 grams) in Persimmon #W and Brick #54.

about felt

There are so many fun and colorful ways to play with felt. The felt that you choose to use for this project could be purchased at a craft store, made from recycled sweaters, or made by hand from wool fleece. 100 percent wool felt or wool blend felts are available at craft and specialty shops, as well as from many online retailers of wool products.

You can make recycled felt from old sweaters by placing them in washing machine with very hot water and a small amount of gentle soap. Fiber contents must be all natural fibers such as wool, mohair, angora, silk, or alpaca. Even a little bit of nylon or synthetic can keep the sweater from felting. Sweaters felt better when they have company—so put several in at a time. Keep in mind, however that colors may run and that lots of lint and fluff appears in the machine as part of the process, so separate darks and lights. Once the sweaters have felted and shrunken to the desired thickness, run them through the rinse and spin, air dry them, and cut them up. If they are not quite the quality you want, try throwing them in the dryer—it's all one big experiment.

Making handmade felt from fleece produces beautiful results, but is a more labor intensive process. For complete instructions on how to make handmade felt from fiber, please refer to the felt-making books and sources listed in the resources section on page 129. These guides will tell you everything you need to know, from what fibers felt best, to what equipment you will need, and more.

Instructions

Loosely CO 90 sts. Work in St St until piece meas about 54" to 56" (137 to 142 cm) from CO edge, or desired length. Loosely BO all sts.

Finishing: Lightly steam block, if necessary. With crochet hook, work 1 row of reverse single crochet ("crab stitch") around all 4 sides. Weave in ends.

Leaves: Using the Autumn Leaf Template on page 28, cut out the desired number of leaves from your leaf background color; the project shown uses 13 leaves. Scatter the leaves randomly on your knitted piece. Sew them in place using a yarn needle and scrap yarn, or with a sewing needle and thread if you prefer. Embellish the leaves as you wish; ours have veins made from brick and persimmon scrap yarn.

Detail of Autumn Leaf

Autumn Leaf Template

do you have enough left to knit across the row?

To make sure that you have enough yarn to get across the row when joining yarn between skeins, the length of yarn remaining should measure at least five or six times the width of the stitches on the needle. To achieve the maximum length possible by using all your available yarn, work until the length of yarn remaining is at least six times the width of the stitches on the needle to ensure that you have enough yarn to bind off.

Wisp of Mist Wrist Warmers

Knitted wrist warmers originated in Scandinavia. Their primary purpose was to provide needed warmth when worn under the cuffs of another garment, but when knit in fancy colors and motifs with interesting and elaborate trims they have also been used as decorative items or status symbols. This quick-to-knit version can add a dainty touch or a surprise of color to any outfit. Let them act as a reminder of the warmth and love of the knitter's craft.

The organic alpaca yarn shown here is incredibly soft and lightweight, so much so that the wrist warmers become a part of you and you might forget you're wearing them. Let them surround your pulse points like a wisp of mist that rises into the cool air from a source of warmth.

FINISHED SIZE: To fit most women
Wrist circumference: 7¾"; (19.5 cm)
Length from deepest point of cast-on edge to bind-off edge: 6"; (15 cm)

YARN: Cottage Industry Pure Luxury Organic Peruvian Alpaca (100% certified organic superfine alpaca; 99 yards [90 meters] /50 grams): 1 skein. Shown in Cream.

▼ *See page 98*

NEEDLES: US 5 (3.75 mm) double-pointed needles (dpn), or size to give gauge.

NOTIONS: Marker, measuring tape, yarn needle, scissors.

GAUGE: 21 sts and 25 rnds = 4" (10 cm) in St St worked in the round (rnd). Check your gauge before you begin.

STITCHES USED:
Stockinette Stitch (St St) Worked in the Round (Rnd): Knit all sts every rnd.

Sl 1 kwise, k2tog, psso: Slip 1 st as if to knit, knit the next 2 sts together, pass the slipped st over as if binding off—3 sts decreased to 1 st.

Lace Pattern (multiple of 10 sts, plus 1)

Rnds 1, 3, 5, and 7: Knit.

Rnd 2: K1, *yo, k3, (sl 1, k2tog, psso), k3, yo, k1; rep from * to end.

Rnd 4: K1, *k1, yo, k2, (sl 1, k2tog, psso), k2, yo, k2; rep from * to end.

Rnd 6: K1, *k2, yo, k1, (sl 1, k2tog, psso), k1, yo, k3; rep from * to end.

Rnd 8: K1, *k3, yo, (sl 1, k2tog, psso), yo, k4; rep from * to end.

Rep these 8 rnds for patt.

NOTE: Take care that you do not accidentally drop or omit a yarnover (yo) that happens to fall at the beginning or end of a needle.

how to make a yarnover

Bring the yarn forward between the needles, and as you knit the next stitch, wrap the yarn over the top of the right-hand needle to create an extra loop on the needle. On the next row, treat this newly created loop like a regular stitch.

Instructions

Loosely CO 41 sts. Join for working in the rnd, being careful not to twist sts, and place marker (pm) to indicate beg of rnd. (See "The Better Join" sidebar on page 32.) Work in Lace Pattern for 16 rnds (two 8-rnd repeats), or longer if desired. Change to St St and work even until piece meas 6" (15 cm) from deepest point of scalloped Lace Pattern, or longer if you have enough yarn. Loosely BO all sts.

Finishing: Weave in ends. Block lightly if desired.

10-st repeat

▲ *Lace Pattern Chart*

	knit on RS
O	yarnover (yo)
⅄	sl 1 kwise, k2tog, psso (see Stitch Guide)

Travel Accessories

Here we have items literally for use in the "air"—travel accessories! The organic cotton aromatherapy eye mask and neck wrap are infused with essential oil to sooth your spirit and ease you into an in-flight nap. Fill the matching drawstring bag with other necessary items to keep you comfortable during a long flight, like your bottled water, lip balm, book, or MP3 player. The amazing organic Peruvian cotton yarn called Pakucho is a joy to use. The colors are "grown into" the cotton itself, which has been cultivated to produce cotton with naturally colored fibers. The allure of this soft, pure, natural product of the earth will make your time in the air more pleasant and enjoyable.

FINISHED SIZES: Travel bag—12" (30.5 cm) wide and 12" (30.5 cm) tall.
Eye mask—10" (25.5 cm) wide and 4" (10 cm) high.
Neck wrap—15" (38 cm) outer diameter and 5" (12.5 cm) wide.

YARN: Cottage Industry Pakucho (100% certified organic cotton; about 95 yards [87 meters]/50 grams)
Travel bag—3 skeins Vanilla (MC), 1 skein each of Café (CC1) and Avocado (CC2).
Eye mask—1 skein each Vanilla (MC) and Café (CC1).
Neck wrap—3 skeins Café (MC), 1 skein each of Vanilla (CC1) and Avocado (CC2).
Entire set—4 skeins Vanilla, 4 skeins Café, and 1 skein Avocado are sufficient to make all three items.

NEEDLES: Travel bag—US 7 (4.5 mm) 16" (40-cm) circular (circ), or size to give gauge. Straight needles in same size for three-needle bind-off.
Eye mask and neck wrap—US 7 (4.5 mm) straight, or size to give gauge.

NOTIONS: Measuring tape, yarn needle, scissors, stitch marker, stitch holder, 2 yards (2 meters) ½" (1.3 cm) coordinating grosgrain ribbon (half each for bag drawstring and eye mask ties), 1 yard (1 meter) cotton

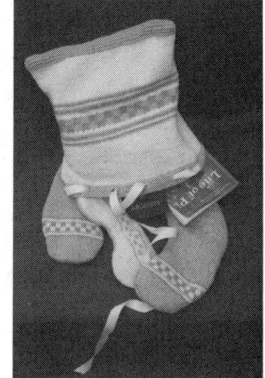

See page 99 ▶

the better join

To avoid having a gap in your work when you begin your first round of circular knitting, knit the first stitch very tightly with the yarn coming from the last stitch cast on. Then continuing knitting around and around until your work is the desired length.

muslin or fine cotton fabric for aromatherapy inserts (¼ for eye mask and ¾ for neck wrap), 2½ cups (625 ml) dried lavender flowers (⅕ for eye mask and ⅘ for neck wrap), 2½ cups (625 ml) whole flax seed (⅕ for eye mask and ⅘ for neck wrap), lavender essential oil (optional). Lavender flowers, flax seed, and essential oil available in natural food stores.

GAUGE: 20 sts and 28 rows = 4" (10 cm) in St St worked flat or in the round (rnd). Check your gauge before you begin.

STITCHES USED:

Stockinette Stitch (St St) Worked in Rows: Knit all sts on RS rows, and purl all sts on WS rows.

Stockinette Stitch (St St) in the Round: Knit all sts every round (rnd).

Three-Needle Bind-Off Technique (See page 19)

TRAVEL BAG

Note: The travel bag is worked upside-down, with the bag opening corresponding to the cast-on edge, and the three-needle bind-off for the bottom of the bag at the top of the knitted piece.

Instructions

With Café and circ needle, CO 120 sts. Join for working in the rnd, being careful not to twist sts, and place marker to indicate beg of rnd. *Purl 1 rnd, knit 1 rnd; rep from * once more, then purl 1 more rnd—5 rnds garter st completed. Eyelet rnd: K4, *yo, k2tog, k8; rep from * 10 more times, end yo, k2tog, k4—12 evenly spaced eyelet holes completed. Purl 1 rnd, knit 1 rnd. Change to Vanilla. Work even in St St for 3" (7.5 cm)—piece meas about 4" (10 cm) from CO edge. Knit 1 rnd each of the foll colors in this order: Café, Avocado, Vanilla, Café, Avocado, Café—6 one-rnd stripes completed. Knit 2 rnds with Vanilla. Work 6 rnds of checkerboard patt as foll:

Rnds 1, 2, and 3: *K3 with Café, k3 with Avocado; rep from * to end.

Rnds 4, 5, and 6: *K3 with Avocado, k3 with café; rep from * to end.

Knit 2 rnds with Vanilla. Knit 1 rnd each of the foll colors in this order: Café, Avocado, Café, Vanilla, Avocado, Café—6 one-rnd stripes completed. With Vanilla, work even in St St until piece meas 11" (28 cm) from CO

edge. Change to Café. *Knit 1 rnd, purl 1 rnd; rep from * 3 more times—8 garter st rnds completed. Carefully turn piece inside out with needle in place, and rearrange sts evenly on 2 straight needles—60 sts each needle. With right sides touching, use three-needle bind-off technique to close bottom of bag.

Finishing: Weave in ends. Cut a 1-yard (1 meter) length of grosgrain ribbon. Trim the ends at a 45-degree angle. Weave ribbon in and out of eyelet holes at top of bag, beg and ending in the center of one flat "face" of the bag.

Eye Mask

Instructions

Lower fronts: With Vanilla and straight needles, CO 10 sts. Work in St St for 6 rows, beg with a RS row, and inc 1 st at each end of every row—22 sts. Place sts on holder. Make a second piece the same as the first.

Join lower fronts: With RS facing, knit across 22 sts on needle, CO 6 sts, return 22 held sts to empty needle with RS facing, knit across 22 sts—50 sts.

Upper front: Work even in St St until piece meas 2¼" (5.5 cm) from CO edge, ending with a WS row. Join Café. Knit 1 row with Café, purl 1 row with Vanilla. Work 4 rows of checkerboard patt as foll:

Row 1: (RS) *K2 with Café, k2 with Vanilla; rep from * to last 2 sts, k2 with Café.

Row 2: *P2 with Café, p2 with Vanilla; rep from * to last 2 sts, p2 with Café.

Row 3: *K2 with Vanilla, k2 with Café; rep from * to last 2 sts, k2 with Vanilla.

Row 2: *P2 with Vanilla, p2 with Café; rep from * to last 2 sts, p2 with Vanilla.

Knit 1 row with Vanilla, purl 1 row with Café. Work in St St with Vanilla for another ½" (1.3 cm), ending with a WS row—piece meas about 4" (10 cm) from CO edge. Purl the next rs row to form turning ridge.

Upper back: Change to Café. Beg and ending with a WS row, work even in St St until piece meas 3" (7.5 cm) from turning ridge, or same length as front between joining row and turning ridge.

Divide lower backs: With RS facing, k22, BO 6 sts, k22 to end—2 groups of 22 sts each.

Lower backs: Working on only one group of 22 sts at a time, work in St St for 6 rows, beg with a WS row, and dec 1 st at each end of every row—10 sts. BO rem sts for this group. Rejoin yarn to second group of sts with WS facing, and work second lower back the same as the first.

Sachet insert: Trace the outline of the mask onto cotton lining fabric, and cut out the insert. Fold insert in half with right sides touching, and with sewing needle and thread, sew along one short side and across curved lower edge with a ¼" (6-mm) seam allowance, leaving rem short side open. Turn insert right side out. Fill with ½ cup (125 ml) dried lavender flowers and ½ cup (125 ml) flax seed. Add several drops of essential oil, if desired. Slipstitch side of insert closed.

Finishing: Weave in ends of mask. Fold mask in half along turning ridge, and with yarn needle and Vanilla, sew along one short side and across the curved lower edge, leaving the rem short side open. Place sachet insert inside mask. With yarn needle and Vanilla, sew rem side of mask closed. Cut a 1-yard (1 meter) length of grosgrain ribbon into two equal halves for ties. Trim one end of each tie at a 45-degree angle. With sewing needle and thread, sew the straight end of each tie to the sides of mask.

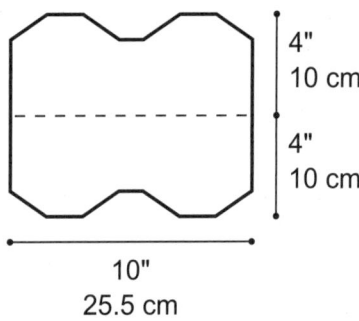

▲ *Eye Mask*

AROMATHERAPY NECK WRAP

Instructions

Back: With Café and straight needles, CO 30 sts. Work in St St for 9 rows, beg and ending with a RS row, and inc 1 st at each end of every row—48 sts. Cont in St St for 26 more rows, beg and ending with a WS row, and inc 1 st at each end of every RS row 13 times—74 sts; piece meas about 5" (12.5 cm) from CO edge.

Dividing row: With RS facing, k28, join second ball of yarn, BO 18 sts, k28 to end—2 groups of 28 sts each. *Note:* The edges on either side of the BO gap are the inner curve edges; with RS facing, the inner curve is at the end of the first group of sts on the needle, and the beg of the second group. The outer edges at each end of the needle are the outer curve edges; with RS facing, the outer curve is at the beg of the first group of sts on the needle, and the end of the second group.

Shape inner curve: Working each side separately, work 1 WS row even. Beg with the next RS row, dec 1 st at each inner curve every RS row 5 times—23 sts at each side. Work even until piece meas 2½" (6.5 cm) from last dec row, about 4" (10 cm) from dividing row, ending with a WS row. On next row, inc 1 st at each inner curve—24 sts at each side. Work 2 rows even. Cont in St St, rep the shaping of the last 3 rows 2 more times—26 sts at each side. On next WS row, inc 1 st at each inner curve—27 sts at each side; piece meas about 5½" (14 cm) from dividing row.

Shape inner and outer curves: Working each side separately, beg with the next RS row, dec 1 st at each outer curve every other row 9 times, and at the same time cont to inc at each inner curve every 3rd row once more—19 sts at each side; piece meas about 8" (20.5 cm) from dividing row when shaping has been completed. Work even in St St until piece meas 9" (23 cm) from dividing row, ending with a WS row.

Shape ends: Working each side separately, beg with the next RS row, dec 1 st at each inner curve every other row 4 times—15 sts; piece meas about 10" (25.5 cm) from dividing row, and about 15" (38 cm) from CO edge. BO all sts at each side.

Front: For solid-color neck wrap, work same as for back. For neck wrap with colorwork motifs shown, work as for back until end of instructions in the "Shape inner curve" paragraph, ending with a WS row—27 sts; piece meas about 5½" (14 cm) from dividing row. Approximate location of colorwork motifs is indicated by dotted lines on the schematic. Work 10 rows in patt from Right and Left charts, increasing at inner curves on Row 3, and dec at outer curves on Rows 1, 3, 5, 7, and 9—23 sts at each side when charts have been completed. Cont in St St with café, dec at outer curve every RS row 4 more times—19 sts at each side; piece meas about 8" (20.5 cm) from dividing row when shaping has been completed. Work even in St St until piece meas 9" (23 cm) from dividing row, ending with a WS row. Work *Shape ends* section same as for back.

Neck wrap: Trace the outline of the neck wrap twice onto cotton lining fabric, and cut out both pieces. Place pieces with right sides touching, and with sewing needle and thread, sew around edges with a ¼" (6-mm) seam allowance, leaving about 3" (7.5 cm) open. Turn insert right side out. Fill with 2 cups (500 ml) dried lavender flowers and 2 cups (500 ml) flax seed. Add several drops of essential oil, if desired. Slipstitch opening closed. If desired, evenly distribute the filling and sew several lines of stitching across the insert through both layers, quilting-fashion, to keep contents in place when neck wrap is worn.

Finishing: Weave in ends of neck wrap. With yarn needle and café, sew back and front tog around all sides, leaving about 6" (15 cm) open along the CO edge. Place insert inside neck wrap. With yarn needle and Café, sew opening closed.

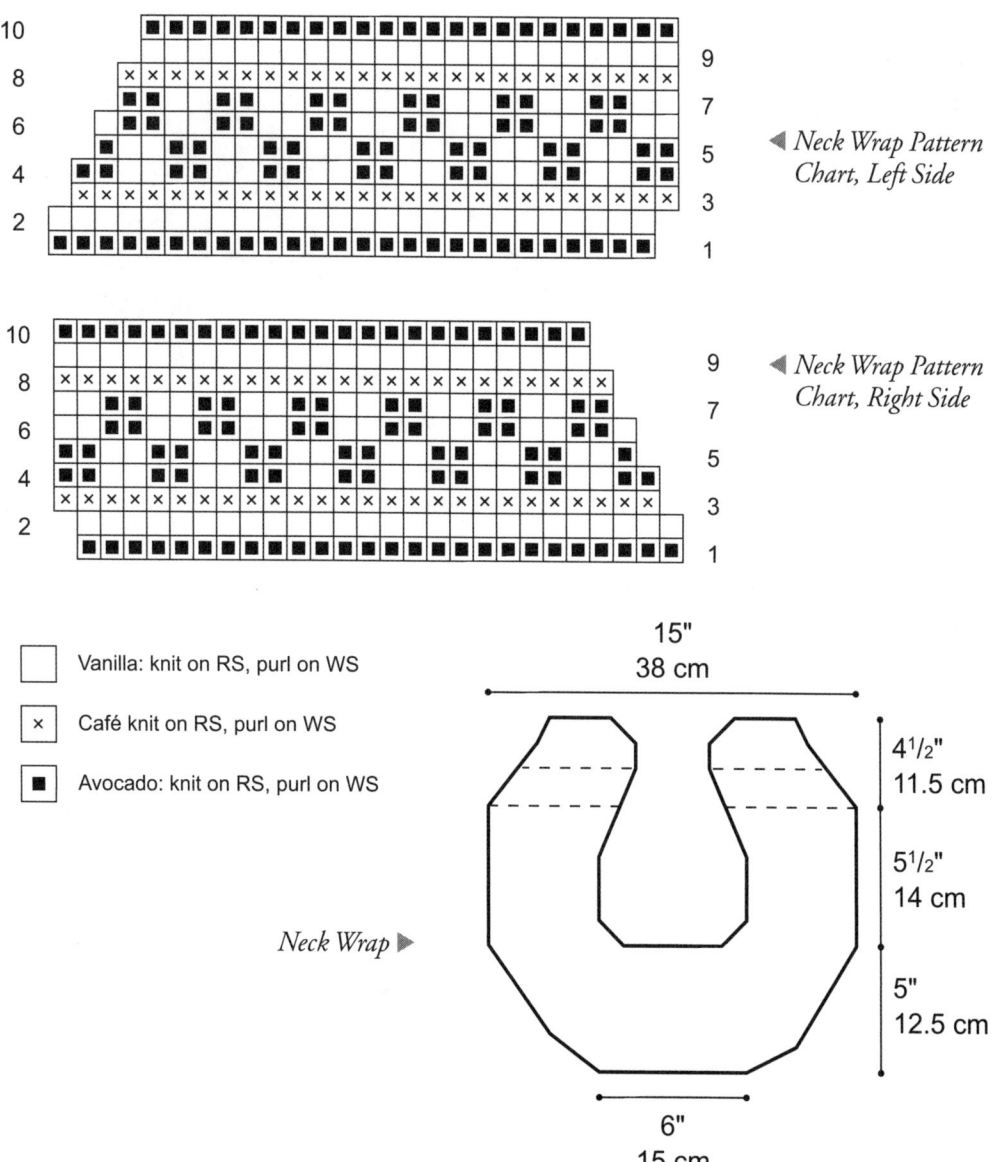

◀ *Neck Wrap Pattern Chart, Left Side*

◀ *Neck Wrap Pattern Chart, Right Side*

Vanilla: knit on RS, purl on WS

× Café knit on RS, purl on WS

■ Avocado: knit on RS, purl on WS

Neck Wrap ▶

15"
38 cm

4¹/₂"
11.5 cm

5¹/₂"
14 cm

5"
12.5 cm

6"
15 cm

ANGELS AND FAIRIES

In our world, angels and fairies often represent the mystical and magical in its purest form. For some, they provide solace and guidance. For others, they open up a realm of play and imagination forgotten since childhood.

Creating angels and fairies can be very transforming in itself. These little beings can often carry a blessing or contain the qualities of certain elements of nature. Creating angels and fairies can be therapeutic, liberating, or just fun. Release your sense of play, and see who comes to be. Develop fairies to represent flowers or develop little friends to offer to someone who is ill or sad. Include both the blessings of your intentions and literal blessings by writing a special verse or prayer on bits of cloth to put inside the fairy. Use your fairies as an exercise in exploring fetishes in the Native American tradition or just make them as little toys to play with and give to special friends.

Make your angels and fairies big or small depending on the weight of yarn and needle size you use. Here, the little fairy is made with a DK weight yarn and the larger angel is made with a light worsted weight yarn, but both use the same pattern and same number of stitches. Play around with different colors and effects by choosing yarns that you find intriguing, or just use what is already in your stash.

FINISHED SIZE: About 5½ (6¾)" (14 [17] cm) tall, not including hair, and 4½ (6)" (11.5 [15] cm) wide at outstretched arms.

◀ *See page 98*

YARN: Fairy—Rowan Wool Cotton (50% wool, 50% cotton; 123 yards [112 meters] /50 grams): 1 skein each for body and dress. Shown in #900 Antique (off-white, for body), #911 Rich (red, for dress).

Angel—Muench Yarns (Horstia) Maulbeerseide-Schurwolle (50% wool, 50% silk; 109 yards [100 meters]/50 grams): 1 skein for body. Shown in #7 Peach.

Crystal Palace Mikado Ribbon (50% cotton, 50% rayon; 112 yards [102 meters]/50 grams): 1 skein for dress. Shown in #1806 Bleached.

Crystal Palace Party Ribbon (100% nylon; 87 yards [80 meters]/50 grams): 1 skein (or partial skein) for sash and hair bows. Shown in #200 Pure White.

NEEDLES: For DK yarn—US 2 (3 mm) straight and set of double-pointed (dpn), or size to give gauge.

For light worsted yarn—US 6 (4 mm) straight and set of dpn, or size to give gauge.

NOTIONS: Measuring tape, yarn needle, scissors, sharp-pointed hand sewing needle, sewing thread to match hair color, embroidery floss in red for mouth and color of choice for eyes, wool roving or scraps of wool yarn for stuffing, locks of unspun fiber or scrap

yarn for hair, ribbon rose for fairy, various materials for wings (feathers, silk flower petals, or leaves). Hair shown: Copper Moth yearling mohair in color Dancing Flame for fairy and undyed natural merino sliver for angel. *Note:* for wings, also consider felt, fabric scraps, dried leaves, or tulle.

GAUGE: For DK yarn—32 sts and 44 rows = 4" (10 cm) in St St.

For light worsted yarn—24 sts and 33½ rows = 4" (10 cm) in St St.

Exact gauge is not critical for this project; just make sure the knitted fabric is nice and tight to prevent stuffing from showing.

STITCHES USED:

Stockinette Stitch (St St): Knit all sts on RS rows, and purl all sts on WS rows.

Make 1 (M1) Increase: Insert the tip of the LH needle from front to back underneath the connecting strand between the two needles, and lift the strand onto the LH needle. Knit the lifted strand through its back loop, twisting it to avoid leaving a hole.

TECHNIQUES USED: Three-Needle Bind-Off Technique (see page 19).

NOTES: Both the DK and light worsted yarn versions are worked over the same number of stitches and rows. When there is a difference in the approximate measurements, the information for the DK version is given first, and the information in parentheses applies to the light worsted version.

The body is worked in one piece, beginning at the back "shoulder blades," and continuing up and over the shoulders to the front, making a centered buttonhole for the neck. The rest of the body and legs are worked from the shoulders down. The schematic shows the body oriented as it will be on your needles, with the legs worked last.

The dress is worked in the round from lower edge of skirt to waist, then divided at the underarms and knit flat to shoulder.

Instructions

Using straight needles given for your yarn weight, CO 36 sts. Work in St St for 7 rows, beg and ending with a WS row.

Neck opening: On the next RS row, k16, BO 4 sts, k16. On the foll WS row, p16, CO 4 sts over gap in previous row, p16—36 sts. Work even for 7 more rows—piece meas about 1½ (2)" (3.8 [5] cm) from CO.

Shape body: At beg of next 2 rows, BO 12 sts—12 sts. At end of next 2 rows, CO 6 sts—24 sts. Work even for 15 more rows, ending with a WS row—piece measures about 3¼ (4¼)" (8.5 [11] cm) from CO.

Legs: On the next RS row, k12 sts, join second ball of yarn, k12 sts. Working each leg separately, work even in St St for 16 rows — piece meas about 4¾ (6¼)" (12 [16] cm) from CO. BO all sts.

Head: Using dpn given for your yarn weight and with RS facing, pick up and knit 4 sts along BO edge of buttonhole, 2 sts at side of neck opening, 4 sts at CO edge of buttonhole, and 2 sts at other side of neck opening—12 sts. Join for working in the round (rnd), and knit one rnd. Increase on next rnd as foll: *K3, M1, rep from * to end—16 sts. Work 10 rnds even. Shape top of head as foll: *K2tog, k2, rep from * to end—12 sts. On the next rnd, work k2tog 6 times—6 sts. Cut yarn leaving an 8" (20-cm) tail, draw through rem sts to secure, and bring yarn tail to inside of head.

Assembly: Stuff head with wool roving or yarn scraps. With yarn needle, sew legs into tubes. Stuff legs. Fold upper body along dotted shoulder line, and sew arms from wrists toward the body. Sew vertical center back seam. Stuff arms and torso. Sew horizontal seam across back between arms. Weave in ends.

Face: With embroidery floss and sewing needle, add mouth and eyes to face. Make mouth with one horizontal running stitch using red, and eyes with two French knots or a few closely spaced horizontal stitches. (See Embroidery Techniques on page 25.)

Hair: Apply roving, fiber locks or scrap yarn to head using sewing needle and matching thread. Apply one lock at a time, referring to the illustration below. Style the hair as desired. I left my fairy's autumn-toned curls loose and flowing. The angel's hair is decorated with bows of Party Ribbon yarn.

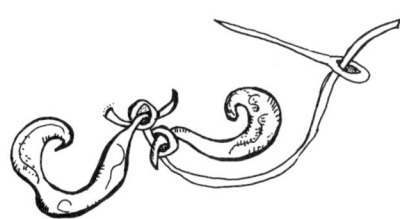

▲ *Fairy Hair*

Apply fairy hair as shown, using a backstitch and catching the lock of fiber or yarn as you secure the stitch. (For backstitch instructions see page 25.)

Dress: Using dpn given for your yarn weight, loosely CO 48 sts. Join for working in the rnd, being careful not to twist. Work in the rnd in St St for about 2 (2½)" (5 [6.5] cm) or desired length for skirt. On the next rnd, work k2tog 24 times—24 sts. Cont work in St St for desired length to underarm; try the dress on doll or hold it up to doll to determine correct length. On the next rnd, divide for front and back as foll: BO 4 sts for armhole, k8 for front, join second ball of yarn, BO 4 sts for other armhole, k8 for back. Working front and back separately, work St St back and forth in rows until bodice is desired length to neck, ending with a WS row—for dresses shown, piece meas about 3½ (4½)" (9 [11.5] cm) from CO for skirt. On the next row, *k2, BO 4 sts at center front for neck, k2; rep from * for back—2 shoulder sts at each side of both front at back. Join front to back at shoulders using three-needle bind-off. Weave in ends. Turn right side out; lower edge of dress will roll to the front. Dress your angel or fairy!

Embellishments: Follow your fancy to embellish your angel or fairy, listening to them to tell you how best to bring out their individual personalities. Each character may represent a different element or strength, or may express a trait of the recipient. I've added a ribbon rose to the front of my fairy's dress, and a sash of Party Ribbon yarn to the angel's.

Wings: Select your wing material. If using feathers, join several at their bases, forming a fan shape, and make two fans the same. Sew the wings together at center with matching sewing thread, and attach to the doll's back. If using silk leaves or petals, place two leaves or petals (or sprigs of either) together to create each wing, then assemble and attach them as for feathers. If you choose to use felt, tulle, or another fabric, cut a pair of wings in your chosen size and shape, and assemble as above.

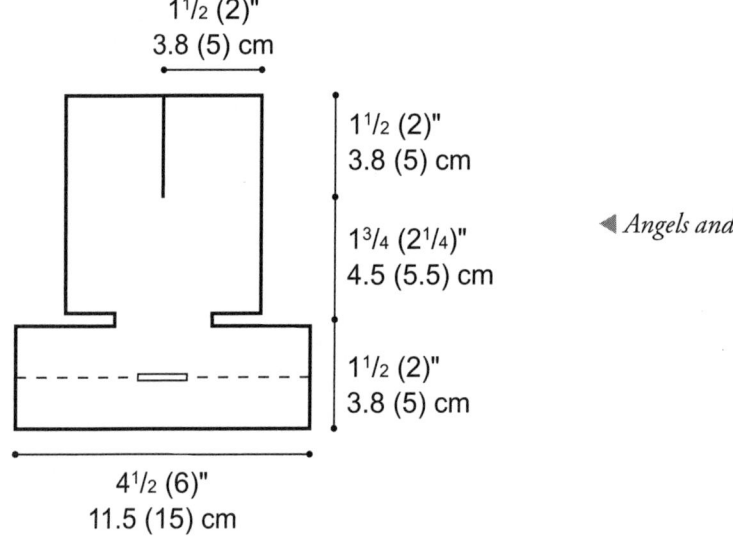

◄ *Angels and Fairies*

part two

EARTH

*Yielding yet solid place your feet firmly on the ground
and take your place with confidence.*

SEA ARAN CARDIGAN

The Aran sweater is a knitted garment born from an amalgamation of knitting styles from fishing cultures up and down the western European seaboard. Yet something about it remains uniquely Irish—so much so that we have come to know this style as "Irish Fisherman" knitting. As is typical of the great Irish story–telling tradition, each stitch in the Aran lexicon tells a tale that is rich in the culture of the sea and the difficult existence of the men and women who lived and died by it.

This slightly flared sweater uses the cable and texture stitches often associated with the sea, and follows the classic Aran sweater structure of arranging the patterns in vertical panels, but also features a contemporary sensibility in its modern styling and shaping. The yarn shown here is a unique cotton-blend, net material with a texture and color that recall the feel and look of sand.

FINISHED SIZE: To fit size 32–34 (36–38, 40–42, 44–46); shown in size 36–38
Chest measurement at underarm: 36 (41, 45½, 50)"; (91.5 [104, 115.5, 127] cm)
Total length: 21½ (23, 24, 25)"; (54.5 [58.5, 61, 63.5] cm)
Sleeve length: 17"; (43 cm) for all sizes

YARN: Crystal Palace Summer Net (45% nylon, 36% polyester, 19% cotton; 74 yards [68 meters]/50 grams): 16 (18, 20, 22) skeins. Shown in #3206 Creamsicle.

See page 100 ▶

NEEDLES: US 11 (8 mm), or size to give gauge.

NOTIONS: Five ½" (1.3 cm) buttons, measuring tape, yarn needle, scissors, stitch holders, cable needle, crochet hook size J/10

folklore of aran stitches

The myths surrounding Aran Knitting are numerous and varied. Some have put forth that the rich cabled patterns of the small islands off Ireland's west coast represent a family or clan, much like the Scottish tartan. Others have suggested that the intertwining and braided stitches harken back to the legendary book of Kells and hold a direct connection to the ornate Celtic stone work of sacred sites and high crosses.

The stitch work of the Aran sweater developed over time through sharing. As a fishing culture, the people of the Aran were part of an international society. As the fleets of different lands moved up and down the western edge of Europe, the people of these areas traded, shared, intermarried, and knit together. The collection of stitches we now know to be Aran knitting are in fact a synthesis of many cultures and folk-knitting traditions that have become distinctive to this one small region. Over time, the textured and cabled patterns began to take on the significance of elements of the islanders' everyday world, and a folklore developed around the imagery attributed to stitch patterns. For example, the Sea Aran includes Irish Moss stitch, Rope Cables, and Trellis stitch. The Irish Moss stitch symbolizes the carrageen seaweed found on the rocky Aran shore and represents fertility and prosperity. The Rope Cables represent the fisherman's ropes and are said to bring good luck to the wearer. They also represent the connection between those who stayed and those who emigrated. The Trellis stitch echoes the decorative elements of Celtic art and jewelry. It symbolizes the fishing nets and the bounty they hold. It also references the hundreds of miles of low stone walls that divide and protect the small, precious fields found on the Islands. Many such meanings accompany the large number of stitches used in Aran knitting. With them knitters can imbue their work with blessings and special meaning. A traditional wedding gift from a mother to a son was a sweater with stitches representing fertility, long life, and the ups and downs of married life. If you try your hand at developing an Aran garment, think about the lineage of knitters who developed the stitches, and how to personalize your knitted masterpiece with wishes and blessing for the wearer. For a more complete list, the Folklore of Aran Stitches can be found on page 125.

(6 mm), stitch markers (optional). Buttons shown: glass buttons from Moving Mud.

GAUGE: 14 sts and 19 rows = 4" (10 cm) in Irish Moss St; 16 sts in Lattice patt from chart meas about 3" (7.5 cm) wide; 8 sts of Right or Left Cross Cable meas about 2" (5 cm) wide. Check your gauge before you begin.

STITCHES USED:

Irish Moss Stitch: (also known as Seed Stitch)
Row 1: (RS) *K1, p1; rep from *, ending k1 if there is an odd number of sts.
All Other Rows: Purl the knit sts, and knit the purl sts as they appear to you.

Right Cable: (worked over 8 sts)
Row 1: (RS) P2, sl next 2 sts to cable needle and hold in back, k2, k2 from cable needle, p2.
Rows 2 and 4: (WS) K2, p4, k2.
Row 3: P2, k4, p2.
Rep these 4 rows for patt.

Left Cable: (worked over 8 sts)
Row 1: (RS) P2, sl next 2 sts to cable needle and hold in front, k2, k2 from cable needle, p2.
Rows 2 and 4: (WS) K2, p4, k2.
Row 3: P2, k4, p2.

Rep these 4 rows for patt.

TECHNIQUES USED: Two-Row, Two-Stitch Buttonhole and Three-Needle Bind-Off Technique (see page 19 for both).

Instructions

Back: Loosely CO 92 (100, 108, 116) sts. Work WS set-up row as foll: Work 6 (10, 14, 18) sts Irish Moss St, [k2, p4, k2] for Cable, *[k2, p4, k4, p4, k2] for Lattice, [k2, p4, k2] for Cable; rep from * two more times, work 6 (10, 14, 18) sts in Irish Moss St. On the next RS row, establish patts as foll, placing markers (pm) if desired between patterns: 6 (10, 14, 18) sts Irish Moss St, *8 sts from Row 1 of Right Cable, 16 sts from Row 1 of Lattice chart; rep from * once more, 8 from Row 1 of Left Cable, 16 sts from Row 1 of Lattice chart, 8 sts from Row 1 of Left Cable, 6 (10, 14, 18) sts Irish Moss St. Cont in patts as established until piece meas ½" (1.3 cm) from CO edge, ending with a WS row. Beg with the next RS row, dec 1 st at each end of needle every 3 (3¼, 3¼, 3½)" (7.5 [8.5, 8.5, 9] cm) four times—84 (92, 100, 108) sts rem; 2 (6, 10, 14) sts at each side in Irish Moss St. Work even, if necessary, until piece meas 13 (13½, 14, 14½)" (33 [34.5, 35.5, 37] cm) from CO edge, ending with a WS row.

Shape armholes: Cont in patts, BO 2 sts at beg of next 2 rows—80 (88, 96, 104) sts. Work even in established patts until armholes meas 7 (8, 8½, 9)" (18 [20.5, 21.5, 23] cm), and piece meas about 20 (21½, 22½, 23½)" (51 [54.5, 57, 59.5] cm) from CO edge, ending with a WS row.

Shape back neck: Work 24 (26, 30, 32) sts in patt, join second ball of yarn, BO center 32 (36, 36, 40) sts, work in patt to end—24 (26, 30, 32) sts at each side for shoulders. Working each side separately, work even until back neck meas 1½" (3.8 cm) from center BO row, and piece meas about 21½ (23, 24, 25)" (54.5 [58.5, 61, 63.5] cm) from CO edge, ending with a WS row. Place sts on holder.

Left front: Loosely CO 44 (48, 52, 56) sts. Work WS set-up row as foll: Work 6 sts Irish Moss St, [k2, p4, k2] for Cable, [k2, p4, k4, p4, k2] for Lattice, [k2, p4, k2] for Cable, work 6 (10, 14, 18) sts in Irish Moss St. On the next RS row, establish patts as foll, pm if desired between patterns: 6 (10, 14, 18) sts Irish Moss St, 8 sts from Row 1 of Right Cable, 16 sts from Row 1 of Lattice chart, 8 sts from Row 1 of Right Cable, 6 sts Irish Moss St. Cont in patts as established until piece meas ½" (1.3 cm) from CO edge, ending with a WS row. Beg with the next RS row, dec 1 st

at side seam edge (beg of RS rows, end of WS rows) every 3 (3¼, 3¼, 3½)" (7.5 [8.5, 8.5, 9] cm) four times—40 (44, 48, 52) sts rem; 2 (6, 10, 14) sts at side seam edge in Irish Moss St. Work even, if necessary, until piece meas 13 (13½, 14, 14½)" (33 [34.5, 35.5, 37] cm) from CO edge, ending with a WS row.

Shape armhole: Cont in patts, BO 2 sts at beg of next RS row—38 (42, 46, 50) sts. Work even in established patts until armhole meas 5½ (6½, 7, 7½)" (14 [16.5, 18, 19] cm), and piece meas about 18½ (20, 21, 22)" (47 [51, 53.5, 56] cm) from CO edge, ending with a RS row.

Shape front neck: At beg of next WS row, BO 14 (16, 16, 18) sts, work in patt to end—24 (26, 30, 32) sts.

Working each side separately, work even until front neck meas 3" (7.5 cm) from neck BO row, and piece meas about 21½ (23, 24, 25)" (54.5 [58.5, 61, 63.5] cm) from CO edge, ending with a WS row. Place sts on holder.

Right front: Loosely CO 44 (48, 52, 56) sts. Work WS set-up row as foll: Work 6 (10, 14, 18) sts Irish Moss St, [k2, p4, k2] for Cable, [k2, p4, k4, p4, k2] for Lattice, [k2, p4, k2] for Cable, work 6 sts in Irish Moss St. On the next RS row, establish patts as foll, pm

intuitive knitting tip: cables as a counter

Basic rope cables provide a convenient natural metronome for your knitting. If your project includes a simple four-stitch by four-row rope cable, you can visually keep track of your pattern by the look of the cable. Rather than trying to count rows when you loose your place—which can be very tricky with cables—try turning the cable. You will know right away if you have turned it too soon or too late. If too soon, work two more rows, if too late, you would have had to rip out a couple of rows no matter what. By working with the cables in a more rhythmic fashion, you start to recognize the meter of right- and wrong-side rows—turning the cables on alternate right-side rows, and coveting your "rest rows" on the wrong side. See if you can integrate this kind of intuitive looseness into your knitting, and relax into your work.

if desired between patterns: 6 sts Irish Moss St, 8 sts from Row 1 of Left Cable, 16 sts from Row 1 of Lattice chart, 8 sts from Row 1 of Left Cable, 6 (10, 14, 18) sts Irish Moss St. Cont in patts as established until piece meas ½" (1.3 cm) from CO edge, ending with a WS row. Beg with the next RS row, dec 1 st at side seam edge (end of RS rows, beg of WS rows) every 3 (3¼, 3¼, 3½)" (7.5 [8.5, 8.5, 9] cm) four times—40 (44, 48, 52) sts rem; 2 (6, 10, 14) sts at side seam edge in Irish Moss St. Work even, if necessary, until piece meas 13 (13½, 14, 14½)" (33 [34.5, 35.5, 37] cm) from CO edge, ending with a RS row.

Shape armhole: Cont in patts, BO 2 sts at beg of next WS row—38 (42, 46, 50) sts. Work even in established patts until armhole meas 5½ (6½, 7, 7½)" (14 [16.5, 18, 19] cm), and piece meas about 18½ (20, 21, 22)" (47 [51, 53.5, 56] cm) from CO edge, ending with a WS row.

Shape front neck: At beg of next RS row, BO 14 (16, 16, 18) sts, work in patt to end—24 (26, 30, 32) sts.

Working each side separately, work even until front neck meas 3" (7.5 cm) from neck BO row, and piece meas about 21½ (23, 24, 25)" (54.5 [58.5, 61, 63.5] cm) from CO edge, ending with a WS row. Place sts on holder.

Shoulder joining: Using Three-Needle Bind-Off Technique (see page 19), join shoulders together, right sides facing, carefully matching left front to left back and right front to right back. The side of the garment with the three-needle bind-off ridge is the WS of the garment.

Sleeves: With RS facing and using crochet hook to assist if desired, pick up 68 (76, 80, 84) sts evenly between armhole notches, with first st picked up at base of notch (notches will be sewn into place later). Work WS set-up row as foll: Work 18 (22, 24, 26) sts Irish Moss St, [k2, p4, k2] for Cable, [k2, p4, k4, p4, k2] for Lattice, [k2, p4, k2] for Cable, work 18 (22, 24, 26) sts in Irish Moss St. On the next RS row, establish patts as foll, pm if desired between patterns: 18 (22, 24, 26) sts Irish Moss St, 8 sts from Row 1 of Right Cable, 16 sts from Row 1 of Lattice chart, 8 sts from Row 1 of Right Cable, 18 (22, 24, 26) sts Irish Moss St. Cont in patts as established until piece meas 2" (5 cm) from CO edge, ending with a WS row. Beg with the next RS row, dec 1 st at each side every 2¼ (2, 1¾, 1¼)" (5.5 [5, 4.5, 3.2] cm) 6 (7, 8, 10) times—56 (62, 64, 64) sts rem; 12 (15, 16, 16) sts at each side

in Irish Moss St. Work even, if necessary, until piece meas 17" (43 cm) from pickup row for all sizes. BO all sts loosely.

Make a second sleeve the same as the first.

Button band: With RS facing and using crochet hook to assist if desired, pick up and knit 64 (70, 72, 76) sts evenly along left front. Work even in Irish Moss St for 6 rows. Loosely BO all sts.

Buttonhole band: With RS facing and using crochet hook to assist if desired, pick up and knit 64 (70, 72, 76) sts evenly along left front. Work even in Irish Moss St for 2 rows. On the next 2 rows, make five buttonholes using the two-row, two-stitch buttonhole method, with the lowest buttonhole ½" (1.3 cm) up from lower edge, the highest ½" (1.3 cm) down from neck edge, and the rem 3 buttonholes about 4⅜ (4¾, 5, 5¼)" (11 [12, 12.5, 13.5] cm) apart. (See Tip for More Intuitive Knitting: Buttonhole Placement on page 93.) Work 2 more rows Irish Moss St. Loosely BO all sts.

Finishing: With crochet hook, work 1 row of single crochet around neck opening. With yarn needle, sew sleeve and side seams. Sew 5 buttons to left front to correspond with buttonhole positions. Weave in ends.

Sea Aran Cardigan ▶

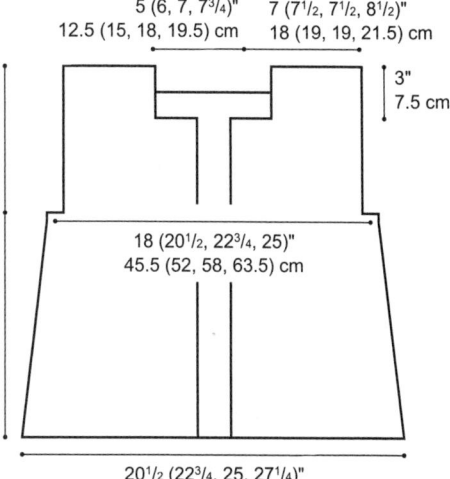

5 (6, 7, 7³/₄)"
12.5 (15, 18, 19.5) cm

7 (7¹/₂, 7¹/₂, 8¹/₂)"
18 (19, 19, 21.5) cm

3"
7.5 cm

8¹/₂ (9¹/₂, 10, 10¹/₂)"
21.5 (24, 25.5, 26.5) cm

18 (20¹/₂, 22³/₄, 25)"
45.5 (52, 58, 63.5) cm

13 (13¹/₂, 14, 14¹/₂)"
33 (34.5, 35.5, 37) cm

20¹/₂ (22³/₄, 25, 27¹/₄)"
52 (58, 63.5, 69) cm

▼ *Lattice Pattern Chart*

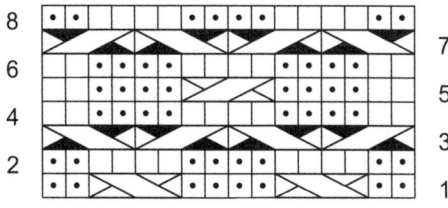

8
6
4
2

7
5
3
1

⬚ knit on RS; purl on WS

[•] purl on RS; knit on WS

place 2 sts on cable needle,
hold in back, k2, k2 from cable needle

place 2 sts on cable needle,
hold in front, k2, k2 from cable needle

place 2 sts on cable needle,
hold in back, k2, p2 from cable needle

place 2 sts on cable needle,
hold in front, p2, k2 from cable needle

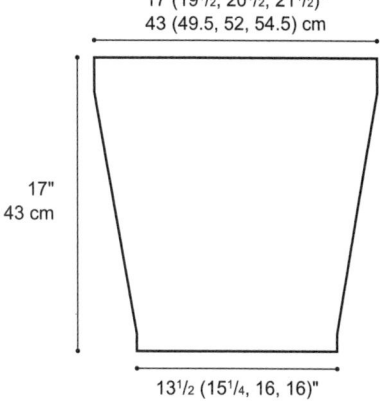

17 (19¹/₂, 20¹/₂, 21¹/₂)"
43 (49.5, 52, 54.5) cm

17"
43 cm

13¹/₂ (15¹/₄, 16, 16)"
34.5 (38.5, 40.5, 40.5) cm

SKY LAKE JACKET

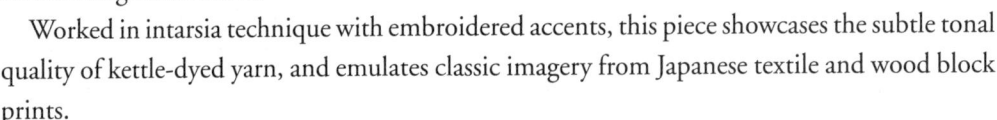

In a moment of stillness, water meets the sky, clouds reflect in the water, and you cannot tell where the earth ends and the sky begins. With this jacket the unity of the natural world is portrayed in swirling water, endless blue sky, maple leaves, blossoms, and the mythic imagery of koi in a still lake. This Japanese-inspired jacket features the rich, deep blues of still and rippling water and reflected sky, with the rich golds and oranges of fleeting carp and floating fallen leaves.

Worked in intarsia technique with embroidered accents, this piece showcases the subtle tonal quality of kettle-dyed yarn, and emulates classic imagery from Japanese textile and wood block prints.

FINISHED SIZE: To fit size 35–37 (40–42); shown in size 40–42
Chest measurement at underarm: 40 (45½)"; (101.5 [115.5] cm)
Total length: 28"; (71 cm) for both sizes
Sleeve length: 17 (18)"; (43 [45.5] cm)

YARN: Manos del Uruguay (100% wool; 137 yards [125 meters]/100 grams): 9 (10) skeins main color (MC); 1 skein each of 4 contrasting colors (CC1, CC2, CC3, and CC4). Shown in #C Powder (medium blue, MC), #39 Cirrus (light blue, CC1), #54 Brick (CC2), #W Persimmon (CC3), and #14

Natural (CC4). *Note:* About ½ skein each of CC2, CC3, and CC4 was used.

NEEDLES: US 7 (4.5 mm) and 9 (5.5 cm) 29" (75-cm) circular (circ), or size to give gauge.

▲ *See page 101*

Two double-pointed needles (dpn) in smaller size for working I-cord ties.

NOTIONS: Measuring tape, yarn needle, scissors, removable markers or safety pins, stitch holders, 4 yards (meters) worsted weight black wool yarn for embroidery, crochet hook size J/10 (6 mm).

GAUGE: 15½ sts and 24 rows = 4" (10 cm) in St St using larger needle. Check your gauge before you begin.

STITCHES USED:
Stockinette Stitch (St St): Knit all sts on RS rows, and purl all sts on WS rows.

TECHNIQUES USED: Three-Needle Bind-Off Technique (see page 19), Intarsia (see page 116).

NOTES: If only one stitch count or measurement is given, it applies to both sizes.

Work motifs from charts in stockinette stitch intarsia, using a different ball of yarn for each color section, and twisting the yarns at each color change to avoid leaving a hole.

The directions for color and placement of the blossoms on each sleeve correspond to the sample jacket shown. Please feel free to work as many blossoms in whatever colors you prefer to make the jacket uniquely your own.

Instructions

Back: With MC and smaller circ, CO 102 (112) sts. Work in garter st (knit all sts every row) for 8 rows—4 garter ridges completed; piece meas about 1" (2.5 cm) from CO edge. Change to larger circ needle and St St, and work even for 2 rows, ending with a WS row. With RS facing, place a removable marker or safety pin after the 14th (19th) and 81st (86th) sts to mark position of Back chart—14 (19) sts before first marker, 67 sts between markers, 21 (26) sts after second marker. *Note:* The Back chart (see pages 60–62) is introduced while the side shaping is in progress; please read the next section all the way through before proceeding. Beg with the next RS row, dec 1 st at each end of needle every 4th row 12 times—78 (88) sts; 2 (7) sts before first marker, 67 sts between markers, 9 (14) sts after second marker. At the same time, when piece meas 2" (5 cm) from CO edge, beg with RS Row 1 of chart, work Back chart over 67 marked sts, working sts on either side of chart section in St St with MC. When side shaping has been completed, work even in patt from chart until piece meas 18" (45.5 cm) from CO edge, ending with a WS row.

Shape armholes: Cont in patt from chart, BO 4 sts at beg of next 2 rows—70 (80) sts. Cont even in patt from chart until Row 145 has been completed. Work even in MC until armholes meas 9¾" (24.5 cm), and piece meas about 27¾" (70.5 cm) from CO edge, ending with a WS row.

Shape back neck: Work 21 (24) sts, join second ball of yarn, BO center 28 (32) sts, work in patt to end—21 (24) sts at each side for shoulders. Working each side separately, work even until piece meas 28" (71 cm) CO edge, ending with a WS row. Place sts on holder.

Right front: With MC and smaller needle, CO 73 (76) sts. Work in garter st (knit all sts every row) for 8 rows—4 garter ridges completed; piece meas about 1" (2.5 cm) from CO edge. Change to larger needle and St St, and work even for 2 rows, ending with a WS row. *Note:* The front shaping cont throughout the side and armhole shaping; please read the next sections all the way through before proceeding. Beg with the next RS row, dec 1 st at side seam edge (end of RS rows) every 4th row 12 times. At the same time, when

piece meas 4" (10 cm) from CO edge, dec 1 st at center front edge (beg of RS rows) every 4th row 36 times. When side shaping has been completed, cont front shaping as established until piece meas 18" (45.5 cm) from CO edge, ending with a RS row.

Shape armhole: Cont front shaping as established, BO 4 sts at beg of next WS row. Cont front shaping until armhole meas 2" (5 cm), and piece meas about 20" (51 cm) from CO edge, ending with a WS row. With RS facing and counting from the end of the row, place markers after the 4th (6th) and 22nd (24th) sts from the end of the row—18 sts between markers, 4 (6) sts at end of row after second marker. Beg with RS Row 1 of chart, work Water Swirl chart (see page 58) with CC1 over 18 marked sts, working sts on either side of chart section in St St with MC. Cont front shaping and patt from chart until Row 30 of chart has been completed. Working the 3 CC1 sts of Row 30 in CC1 to end, work rem sts in MC until front shaping has been completed— 21 (24 sts). Work even until armhole meas 10" (25.5 cm), and piece meas 28" (71 cm) CO edge, ending with a WS row. Place sts on holder.

Left front: With MC and smaller needle, CO 73 (76) sts. Work in garter st (knit all sts every row) for 8 rows—4 garter ridges completed; piece meas about 1" (2.5 cm) from CO edge. Change to larger needle and St St, and work even for 2 rows, ending with a WS row. With RS facing, place a removable marker or safety pin after the 4th and 54th sts to mark position of Koi chart—4 sts before first marker, 50 sts between markers. *Note:* The Koi chart (see page 62) is introduced while the side and front shaping are in progress, and the front shaping cont throughout the piece as for left front; please read the next sections all the way through before proceeding. Beg with the next RS row, dec 1 st at side seam edge (beg of RS rows) every 4th row 12 times. At the same time, when piece meas 2" from CO edge, beg with RS row 1 of chart, work sts before marked chart section in CC1, work Koi chart over 50 marked sts, work to end with MC. For Rows 1-8 of chart, work sts between chart and side edge in CC1; after Row 8 work all sts on either side of chart in MC. Also at the same time, when piece meas 4" (5 cm) from CO edge, dec 1 st at center front edge (end of RS rows) every 4th row 36 times. When side shaping has been completed, cont front shaping and chart as established until Row 62 of chart has been completed. With MC, cont front shaping until piece meas 18" (45.5 cm) from CO edge, ending with a WS row.

Shape armhole: Cont front shaping as established, BO 4 sts at beg of next RS row. Cont in MC, until front shaping has been completed—21 (24 sts). Work even, if necessary, until armhole meas 10" (25.5 cm), and piece meas 28" (71 cm) CO edge, ending with a WS row. Place sts on holder.

Shoulder joining: Using three-needle bind-off technique (see page 19), join shoulders together, right sides facing, carefully matching left front to left back and right front to right back. The side of the garment with the three-needle bind-off ridge is the WS of the garment.

Left sleeve: With RS facing and using crochet hook to assist if desired, using larger needle and MC, pick up 86 sts evenly between armhole notches, with first st picked up at base of notch (notches will be sewn into place later). With RS facing, place a removable marker or safety pin in the exact center of the row—43 sts on either side of marker. *Note:* The Blossom chart (see page 58) is introduced 3 different times while the sleeve shaping is in progress; please read the next section all the way through before proceeding. Work in St St until piece meas 1" (2.5 cm) from pickup row, ending with a WS row Beg with the next RS row, dec 1 st at each end of needle every

4th row 20 times—46 sts rem when sleeve shaping has been completed. At the same time, when piece meas 2" (5 cm) from pickup row, beg with RS Row 1 of chart, work Blossom chart using CC3 over 13 sts, beg 6 sts before and ending 7 sts after the center marker, working sts on either side of chart section in St St with MC. Cont sleeve shaping and work until Row 15 of chart has been completed. With MC, cont side shaping until piece meas 8" (20.5 cm) from pickup row, ending with a WS row. Beg with RS Row 1 of chart, work Blossom chart using CC1 over 13 sts, beg 19 sts before and ending 6 sts before the center marker, working sts on either side of chart section in St St with MC. Cont sleeve shaping and work until Row 15 of chart has been completed. With MC, cont side shaping until piece meas 13½ (14½)" (34.5 [37] cm) from pickup row, ending with a WS row. Beg with RS Row 1 of chart, work Blossom chart using CC4 over 13 sts, beg 5 sts before and ending 8 sts after the center marker, working sts on either side of chart section in St St with MC. When Row 15 of chart has been completed, purl 1 WS row with MC, dec 4 sts evenly—42 sts. Change to smaller needle and work in garter st until piece meas 17 (18)" (43 [45.5] cm) from pickup row. Loosely BO all sts.

Right sleeve: Pick up and knit 86 sts, marking center of row as for left sleeve. *Note:* Sleeve shaping begins at same time as first blossom motif; please read the next section all the way through before proceeding. Work as for left sleeve until piece meas 1" (2.5 cm) from pickup row. Beg with the next RS row, dec 1 st at each end of needle every 4th row 20 times as for left sleeve—46 sts rem when sleeve shaping has been completed. Also at the same time, when piece meas 1" (5 cm) from pickup row, beg with RS Row 1 of chart, work Blossom chart using CC4 over 13 sts, beg 5 sts after and ending 18 sts after the center marker, working sts on either side of chart section in St St with MC. Cont sleeve shaping and work until Row 15 of chart has been completed, then work 1 WS row. Beg with RS Row 1 of chart, work Blossom chart using CC1 over 13 sts, beg 12 sts before and ending 1 st after the center marker, working sts on either side of chart section in St St with MC. Cont sleeve shaping and work until Row 15 of chart has been completed. With MC, cont side shaping until piece meas 12½ (13½)" (31.5 [34.5] cm) from pickup row, ending with a WS row. Beg with RS Row 1 of chart, work Blossom chart using CC2 over 13 sts, beg 9 sts before and ending 4 sts after the center marker, working sts on either side of chart section in St St with MC. When Row 15 of chart has been completed, work until piece meas same as left sleeve from pickup row to beg of garter st edging, ending with a RS row. Purl 1 WS row with MC, dec 4 sts evenly—42 sts. Change to smaller needle and work in garter st for same number or rows as left sleeve. Loosely BO all sts.

Embroidery: With yarn needle, work long straight sts and French knots to embellish center of sleeve blossoms according to detail below. With yarn needle and CC3, work leaf veins in backstitch on leaf from Back chart. With yarn needle and CC3, outline koi fins using backstitch as shown. Using black worsted wool, embroider pupils on koi's eyes. Secure all ends. (See Embroidery Techniques on page 25.)

▲ *Detail of Blossom Embroidery*

Front band: With MC, RS facing and smaller needle. using crochet hook if desired, starting at beg of right front neck shaping, pick up and knit 90 sts along shaped right front edge to shoulders, 4 sts at right side of back neck, 26 (30) sts across back neck, 4 sts at left side of back neck, and 90 sts along shaped edge of left front to end at beg of left front shaping—214 (218) sts. Work even in garter st until front band meas 1½" (3.8 cm) from pickup row, or desired length. BO all sts loosely as if to knit.

Center front edges: With MC and RS facing, use crochet hook to work 1 row of single crochet along 4" (10-cm) straight section on either side of front opening from CO edge to beg of front band.

Finishing: With yarn needle, sew sides of 1" (2.5 cm) sleeve extensions to sleeve notches. Sew sleeve and side seams. Meas up 6" (15 cm) from CO edge along right side seam and place removable marker or safety pin. With MC and RS facing, with dpn pick up and knit 3 sts at marked position on seam. Work in I-cord for 6" (15 cm) or desired length of tie. Cut yarn leaving 8" to 10" (20- to 30-cm) tail, draw through rem sts, pull snugly to close end of cord, and bring yarn tail to inside of cord. Work 3 more ties in the same manner in the foll locations: at corner of right front band, at corner of left front band, and on inside of left side seam 6" (15 cm) up from CO edge. Weave in ends. Steam block lightly if needed. To wear, tie right front to inside left side seam, lap left front over right, and tie left front to right side seam.

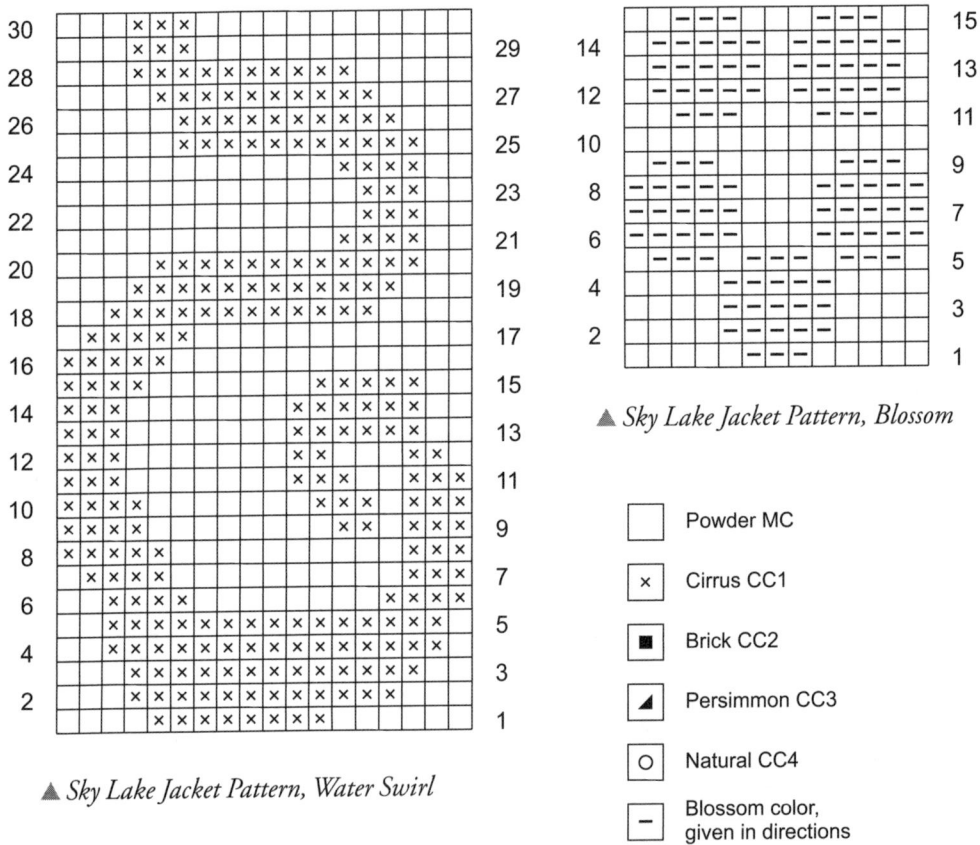

▲ *Sky Lake Jacket Pattern, Water Swirl*

▲ *Sky Lake Jacket Pattern, Blossom*

	Powder MC
×	Cirrus CC1
■	Brick CC2
◢	Persimmon CC3
○	Natural CC4
−	Blossom color, given in directions

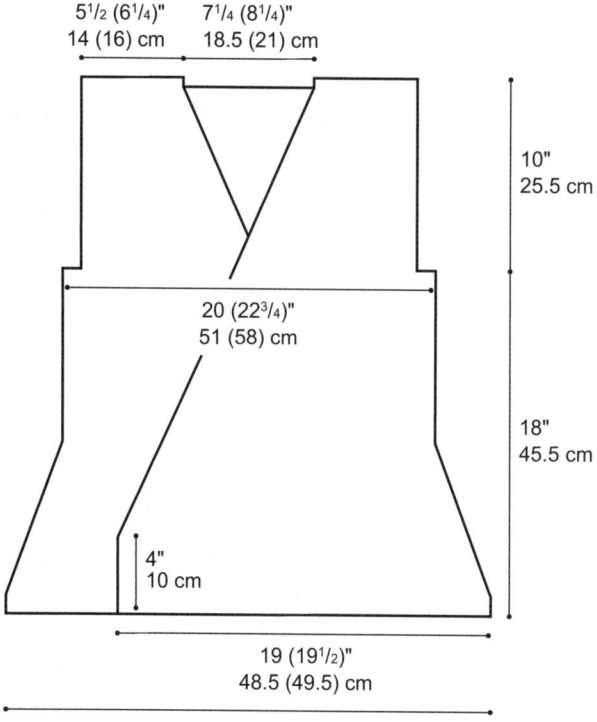

5¹/₂ (6¹/₄)" 7¹/₄ (8¹/₄)"
14 (16) cm 18.5 (21) cm

10"
25.5 cm

20 (22³/₄)"
51 (58) cm

18"
45.5 cm

4"
10 cm

19 (19¹/₂)"
48.5 (49.5) cm

26¹/₂ (29)"
67.5 (73.5) cm

◀ *Sky Lake Jacket*

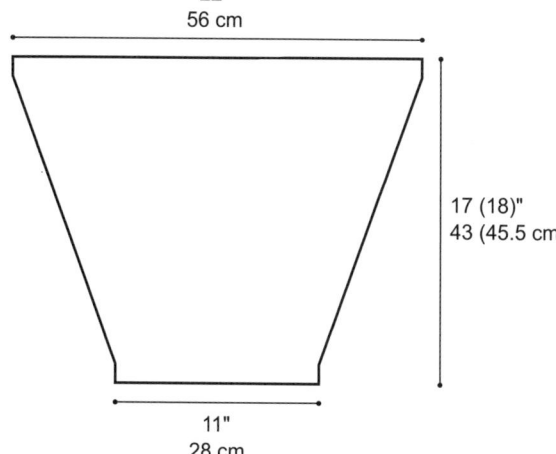

22"
56 cm

17 (18)"
43 (45.5 cm

11"
28 cm

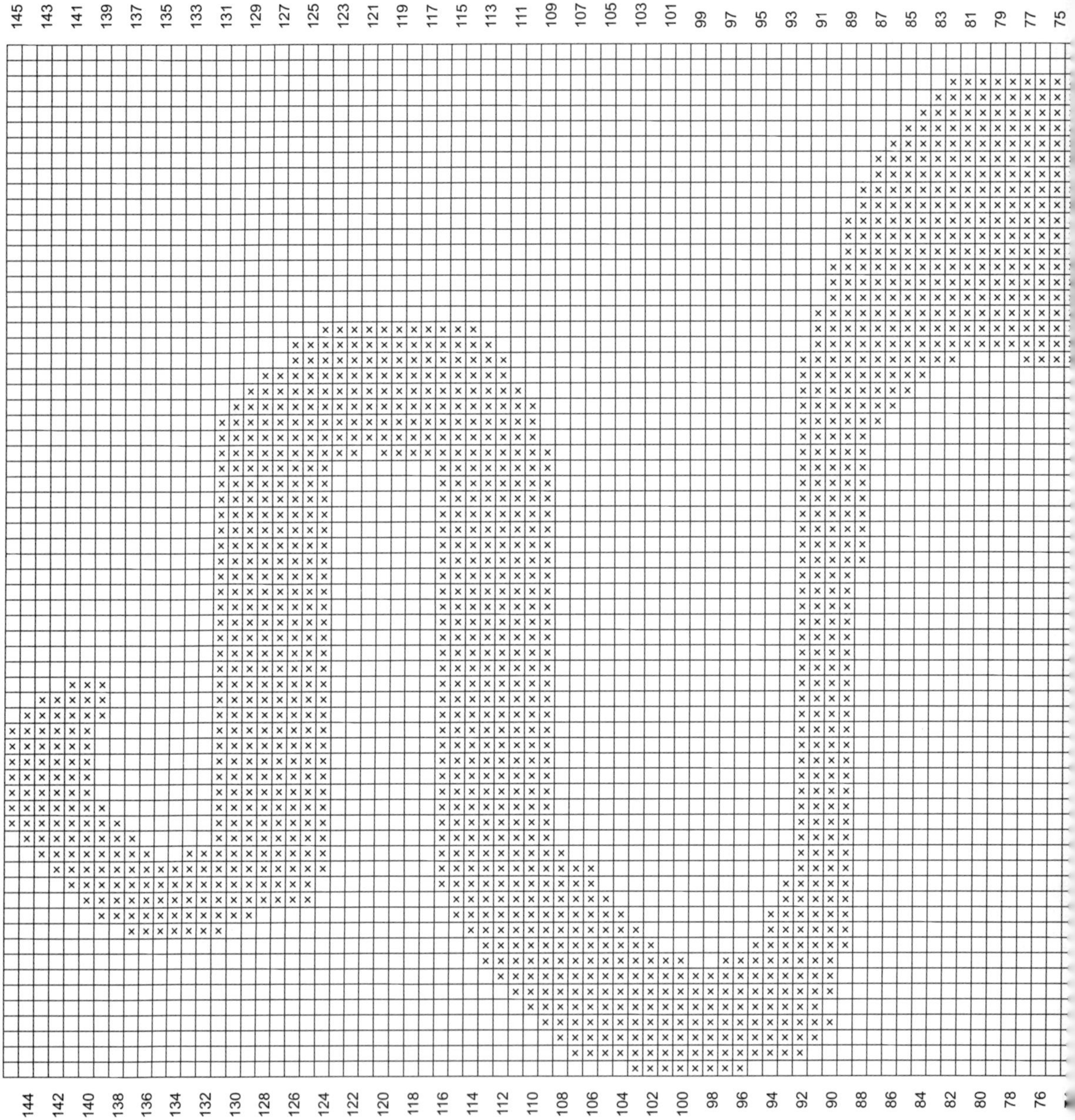
145 143 141 139 137 135 133 131 129 127 125 123 121 119 117 115 113 111 109 107 105 103 101 99 97 95 93 91 89 87 85 83 81 79 77 75
144 142 140 138 136 134 132 130 128 126 124 122 120 118 116 114 112 110 108 106 104 102 100 98 96 94 92 90 88 86 84 82 80 78 76

▲ *Sky Lake Jacket Pattern, Back*

▲ *Sky Lake Jacket Pattern, Koi*

Snowfall Wrap

The beauty found in a virgin blanket of freshly fallen snow makes the world seem a little smaller and very quiet. This still, silent quality reflects the place within ourselves where we can find mindfulness—a moment of being aware of yourself and your surroundings without judgment.

The Snowfall Wrap manifests the surface, color, and quality of fresh snow on the ground using a combination of textured novelty yarns with a base of wool yarn. You can literally wrap yourself in this piece to protect you from the snowfall or to explore the metaphors it can offer—undisturbed beauty, contemplative space, warmth, and unexplored territory.

Finished Size: About 10" (25.5 cm) wide and 73" (185.5 cm) long, not including fringe.

◀ *See page 103*

Yarn: Crystal Palace Iceland (100% wool; 109 yards [100 meters]/100 grams): 3 skeins. Shown in #1058 New Snow.
Crystal Palace Dragonfly (70% polyester, 30% nylon; 44 yards [40 meters]/50 grams): 3 skeins. Shown in #0204 White White
Crystal Palace Raggedy (50% acrylic, 30% nylon, 20% wool; 56 yards [51 meters]/50 grams): 3 skeins. Shown in #2182 Ivory White.

Needles: US 13 (9 mm) 32" (80-cm) or longer circular (circ) needle, or size to give gauge.

NOTIONS: Measuring tape, yarn needle, scissors.

GAUGE: About 11 sts and 16 rows = 4" (10 cm) in garter stitch (knit all sts every row) using Iceland. Exact gauge is not critical for this project.

STITCHES USED:

Seed Stitch (worked over an even number of sts)

Row 1: *K1, p1; rep from * to end.
Row 2: *P1, k1; rep from * to end.
Rep these 2 rows for patt.

NOTE: As you change yarns, leave a 5" (12.5-cm) tail of both the old and new yarns at the beginning of the row. These ends will be knotted together later for fringe.

For a wider wrap, purchase more yarn and work until desired width.

Instructions

With Iceland, loosely CO 200 sts, and knit 4 rows. Work textured patt as foll:

Rows 1–2: With Dragonfly, knit 2 rows.
Rows 3–6: With Raggedy, work 4 rows Seed St.
Rows 7–8: With Dragonfly, knit 2 rows.
Rows 9–12: With Iceland, knit 4 rows.
Rep Rows 1–12 until wrap meas 10" (25.5 cm) from CO edge, or desired width, ending with Row 11. With Iceland, BO all sts loosely as if to knit.

Finishing: Knot the tails at each short end of wrap for fringe. To add more fringe, cut 12" (30-cm) lengths of leftover yarn. Fold each length in half, poke folded loop through edge of wrap, and draw the two tails through the loop to secure. Trim the ends of the new fringes even with the knotted 5" (12.5-cm) tails of the original fringe.

Black Sand Haori Vest

One of the most breathtaking sights I have ever seen is the black sand beaches of the Hawaiian Islands. The extremes of deep blue ocean water, white sea foam, and black sand that sparkles like diamonds provides an unmistakable reminder that you are perched at the edge of an ancient lava flow.

This Japanese Haori (wrap-style vest) with a single tie closure features yarns and stitches that unite the shimmering and gritty effects of black sand. The elegant red trim reminds us of the volcanic source of these amazing sands, and serves as a metaphor for the liquid core of the earth, individuals, or different situations—either soft or molten, depending on what or whom.

FINISHED SIZE: Woman's S (M, L, XL); shown in size XL

Chest measurement: 37 (42, 47, 52)"; (94 [106.5, 119.5, 132] cm)

Total length from lower edge to shoulders: 24 (25, 26, 27)"; (61 [63.5, 66, 68.5] cm)

Note: Chest measurement is with fronts hanging straight down, with a 3½ (4, 4½, 5)" (9 [10, 11.5, 12.5] cm) gap at center front; when vest is tied so that fronts meet in the middle, the measurement will be slightly smaller at the bust than the hips.

YARN: Colinette Zanziba (50% wool, 50% viscose; 98 yards [90 meters]/100 grams): 4 (5, 6, 7) skeins main color (MC). Shown in #BLK Black.

Crystal Palace Cotton Chenille (100% cotton; 108 yards [98 meters]/50 grams): 1 (2, 2, 2) skeins contrast color (CC). Shown in #8166.

▲ *See page 99*

NEEDLES: US 8 (5 mm) and US 10 (6 mm) 29" (75-cm) circular (circ), or size to give gauge on larger needle. *Note:* You may find it helpful to use a pair of US 8 (5 mm) double-pointed needles (dpn) for making the front ties.

NOTIONS: Measuring tape, yarn needle, scissors, safety pins or scrap yarn, crochet hook size J/10 (6 mm; optional).

GAUGE: 14 sts and 22 rows = 4" (10 cm) in St St using Zanziba with larger needle. Check your gauge before you begin.

STITCHES USED:
Stockinette Stitch (St St): Knit all sts on RS rows, and purl all sts on WS rows.

NOTE: Body is worked in one piece starting at the lower back edge and working to the shoulders, then the piece divides into two fronts that are worked from the shoulders down to the lower front edges.

Instructions

Back: With MC and larger needle, CO 53 (60, 68, 75) sts. Work in St St until piece meas 24 (25, 26, 27)" (61 [63.5, 66, 68.5] cm) from CO edge, ending with a WS row.

Fronts: On next RS row, work across 14 (16, 20, 23) sts, join second ball of yarn and BO center 25 (28, 28, 29) sts for back neck, work to end—14 (16, 20, 23) sts at each side. Work even until piece meas 24 (25, 26, 27)" (61 [63.5, 66, 68.5] cm) from back neck BO, or 48 (50, 52, 54)" (122 [127, 132, 137] cm) from CO edge. BO all sts.

Side panels: Measure up 12½ (13, 13½, 14)" (31.5 [33, 34.5, 35.5] cm) from lower edge along the side edge of each front and both sides of the back, and mark the positions with safety pins or scrap yarn to indicate beg of armholes. With MC, larger needle, and RS facing, using crochet hook to assist if desired, pick up and knit 44 (45, 47, 49) sts along side of left front between lower edge and armhole marker. Work in St St for 3½ (4, 4, 4½)" (9 [10, 10, 11.5] cm). BO all sts. Work a second side panel in the same manner on the side edge of the right front, picking up from the armhole marker to the lower edge. With yarn needle, sew bound-off edges of side panels to sides of back between the markers.

Armhole edging: With CC, smaller needle, and RS facing, beg at base of armhole, pick up and knit 40 (42, 44, 46) sts from base of armhole to shoulder line, 40 (42, 44, 46) sts from shoulder line to base of armhole, and 12

(14, 14, 16) sts along top of side panel—92 (98, 102, 108) sts. Do not join. Knit 1 row. BO all sts loosely as if to knit; you may wish to use a needle one or two sizes larger for binding off.

Front and neck band: Measure up 14½ (15, 15½, 16)" (37 [38, 39.5, 40.5] cm) from lower edge along both sides of front opening, and mark the positions with safety pins or scrap yarn to indicate position for neckband color change. With MC, smaller needle, and RS facing, pick up and knit 50 (52, 54, 56) sts from lower edge of right front opening to marker, change to CC, pick up and knit 33 (35, 37, 39) sts from marker to shoulder line, 25 (28, 28, 29) sts across back neck, 33 (35, 37, 39) sts from shoulder line to marker, change to MC (join a new ball of MC), pick up and knit 50 (52, 54, 56) sts from marker to lower edge of left front—191 (202, 210, 219) sts. Knit 14 rows in colors as established, twisting yarns at color changes to avoid leaving holes as you would for intarsia

knitting—band meas about 1¾" (4.5 cm) from pickup row. BO all sts loosely as if to knit; you may wish to use a needle one or two sizes larger for binding off.

Front ties: With CC, smaller needle (either circ or 2 dpn), and RS facing, pick up and knit 3 sts at edge of front band at color join. Work I-cord for 8" (20.5 cm) or desired length. Cut yarn leaving an 8" (20-cm) tail, draw through all sts, pull snugly to close end of I-cord, and bring yarn tail to inside of tie.

Finishing: Weave in ends.

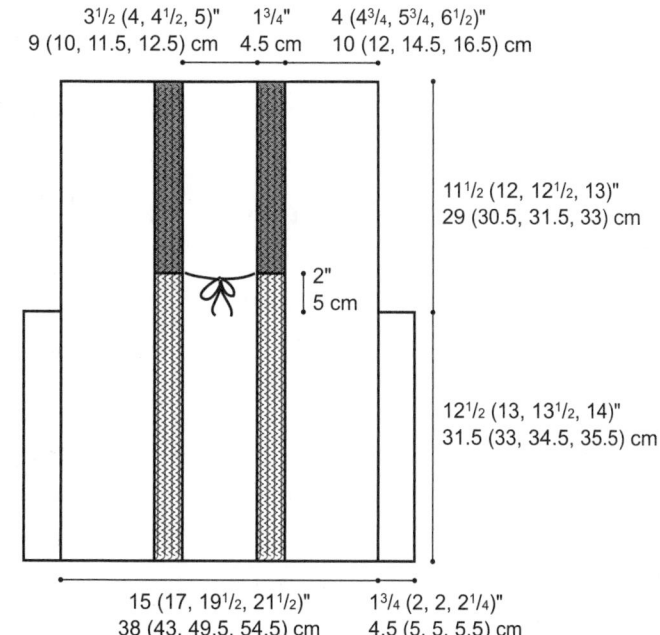

3½ (4, 4½, 5)"   1¾"   4 (4¾, 5¾, 6½)"
9 (10, 11.5, 12.5) cm   4.5 cm   10 (12, 14.5, 16.5) cm

11½ (12, 12½, 13)"
29 (30.5, 31.5, 33) cm

2"
5 cm

12½ (13, 13½, 14)"
31.5 (33, 34.5, 35.5) cm

Black Sand Vest ▶

15 (17, 19½, 21½)"   1¾ (2, 2, 2¼)"
38 (43, 49.5, 54.5) cm   4.5 (5, 5, 5.5) cm

WALKING MEDITATION SOCKS

These warm cozy socks are for keeping toes toasty or for literally feeling the earth while walking on the ground. A basic sock pattern is offered here with a "knot of eternity" motif worked in a contrasting color. This interlacing knot design appears in spiritual traditions throughout the world, and is most often associated with Buddhist and Celtic symbolism. We offer two versions here—one in Celtic slate blue and natural gray, and the other in a rich burgundy and gold inspired by Buddhist monk's robes. These socks make great gifts for keeping the feet warm during hours of sitting practice and actual walking mediation, or as a whimsical addition to your favorite clogs or walking shoes.

FINISHED SIZE: Woman's medium (man's medium); to fit a woman's US shoe size 7–9 (man's US shoe size 9–10½); shown in woman's medium
Foot length: 9½ (10½)"; (24 [26.5] cm)
Foot circumference: 8 (9½)"; (20.5 [24] cm)
Length to top of heel: 7½ (9)"; (19 [23] cm)

See page 103 ▶

YARN: Mostly Merino Sport Singles (77% Merino and Corriedale wool, 23% mohair); 250 yards [229 meters]/2 ounces/[57 grams]): 2 (3) skeins main color (MC); 1 (1) skein or about 100 yards (91 meters) contrast color (CC). Shown in Pema's Purple (MC) with Tansy (CC) for monk's robe colorway, and Slate Blue (MC) with Natural (CC) for Celtic colorway.

NEEDLES: US 2 (3 mm) double-pointed needles (dpn), or size to give gauge.

NOTIONS: Removable markers, measuring tape, yarn needle, scissors, 4 yards [3.5 meters] smooth scrap yarn.

GAUGE: 30 sts and 44 rows = 4" (10 cm) in St St worked in the round (rnd). Check your gauge before you begin.

walking meditation

Walking meditation provides the mindfulness practitioner with a way to break up periods of sitting meditation and with a method of mindfulness practice that can be used on its own to expand awareness to the entire body and out into the environment.

Walking meditation may offer a break during a period of sitting meditation or mindful knitting. When we can stretch our legs and get the circulation going, and during a long period of sitting meditation you may find yourself eagerly anticipating the next walking break—a change of activity, a bit of entertainment, a time to integrate mind and body.

The basic element of walking meditation is the shift of the object of focus from the flow of breath to the movement of footfall. When practiced in conjunction with sitting meditation, the meditator stands and walks in a small circle around the room, very deliberately focusing on the sensation of the feet contacting the floor, and the subtlety of the transfer weight from heel to toe, from foot to foot.

When used as a form of meditation on its own, walking meditation can be a beautiful way to engage with nature and the environment. It allows us to wake up our senses and notice nuances that we might otherwise miss in the noise of our minds. You can use walking meditation while on a hike or on your way to work. Begin with your focus on the process of walking—the movement of your feet and the sensation of motion. Once you have rested your mind into the pattern of your steps, you may expand your awareness slightly outward, noticing a sound, and placing your focus there. Then, you may again expand out further, paying attention to the sky. As your focus expands, continue to hold your attention very deliberately on the object with which you choose to connect. If your attention wanders, and your mind begins to fill up, use the labeling technique, gently reminding yourself that you are thinking, and bring your focus back to the simple placement of your feet as you walk, the shifting of your weight, and the essential quality of being on the earth.

STITCHES USED:

K2, P2 Rib (multiple of 4 sts)

All rnds: *K2, p2; rep from * to end.

Stockinette Stitch (St St) Worked in the Round (Rnd): Knit all sts every rnd.

Kitchener Stitch: Please refer to a knitting reference book for information on this technique (see the Bibliography and Further Reading on page 131).

NOTE: For a nice, stretchy cast-on edge, consider casting on all stitches over 2 double-pointed needles held together. Then remove one needle and divide the stitches evenly onto three needles for working.

Instructions

Cuff: With MC, loosely 60 (72) sts with MC. Join for working in the rnd, being careful not to twist sts, and place marker (pm) to indicate beg of rnd. Work even in k2, p2 rib until piece meas 3 (4)" (7.5 [10] cm) from CO or desired length for cuff.

Leg: Change to St St, and cont with MC until piece meas 7½ (9)" (19 [23] cm) from CO or desired length to top of heel. On the next rnd, work sts for afterthought heel as foll: Work 24 (28) sts with MC, cut MC leaving a 6" to 8" (15- to 20-cm) tail, work 36 (44) sts with scrap yarn, rejoin MC leaving a 6" to 8" (15- to 20-cm) tail.

Foot: Cont in St St with MC until piece measures 5" (12.5 cm) from scrap yarn for both sizes, or 4½ (5½)" (11.5 [14] cm) less than desired total foot length. The toe will add 2 (2½)" (5 [6.5] cm) and the heel will add 2½ (3)" (6.5 [7.5] cm) to overall length.

Toe: Before beg the next rnd, rearrange sts on 3 needles as foll: 15 (18) sts on needle 1, 30 (36) sts on needle 2 for instep, and 15 (18) sts on needle 3. Change to CC. Shape toe as foll:

Rnd 1: On needle 1, knit to last 3 sts, k2tog, k1; on needle 2, k1, ssk, knit to last 3 sts, k2tog, k1; on needle 3, k1, ssk, knit to end—4 sts decreased.

Rnd 2: Knit.

Rep these 2 rnds 7 (10) more times—28 sts rem for both sizes. Work Rnd 1 only 4 more times—12 sts rem for both sizes. Knit the sts from needle 1 onto the end of needle 3—6 sts each on two needles, one each for top and sole of foot. Cut yarn, leaving a 12" to 18" (30- to 45-cm) tail. Graft sts of toe closed using Kitchener Stitch.

Heel: The afterthought heel is essentially a second toe worked outwards from the scrap yarn placeholder. This method allows the heel to be easily unraveled and re-knit if it wears out.

Carefully remove the scrap yarn to expose "live" sts at the top and bottom of the heel opening. Place these sts on 2 dpn as they become free, one needle each for top and bottom of the opening—72 (88) sts total, 36 (44) sts each for top and bottom. Rearrange sts on 3 needles as foll, beg with the center of the bottom needle: 18 (22) sts on needle 1 for half of sole, 36 (44) sts on needle 2 for upper back edge of heel, and 18 (22) sts on needle 3 for other half of sole. Join CC at beg of needle 1; rnd begins at in the middle of the bottom of the foot. Knit 3 rnds. Rep Rnds 1–2 of toe 11 (15) times—28 sts rem for both sizes. Work Rnd 1 only 4 more times—12 sts rem for both sizes. Knit the sts from needle 1 onto the end of needle 3—6 sts each on two needles, one each for top and bottom of heel. Cut yarn, leaving a 12" to 18" (30- to 45-cm) tail. Graft sts of heel closed using Kitchener Stitch. Weave in ends.

Knot motif: Fold the sock in half with the fold lines at the exact back and front of the leg so that the foot lies flat with the toe in profile.

Determine where you would like to place the motif. To position the knot on the front of the leg as shown, meas down along center front fold approximately 3½ (4½)" (9 [11.5] cm) from CO edge at top of cuff, and place a removable marker between the 2 sts at center front. Count out 4 sts from the center at each side and place 2 more markers. Remove the center marker—8 sts between rem 2 markers. These 8 sts correspond to the center 8 sts for Row 1 of Knot Motif chart (see page 72), which will be worked upwards toward the cuff from this point. Using a yarn needle and CC, work sts from Row 1 of chart in duplicate stitch to establish the "base" of the motif. *Note:* You may find it helpful to stretch the sock over a cylindrical object like a soda bottle when working embroidery; it will also help to prevent you from working the duplicate stitching too tightly which can interfere with the stretchiness of the sock. Cont working duplicate stitch until all rows of chart have been completed. Secure all ends.

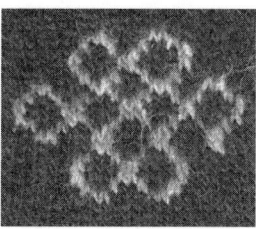

◀ *Detail of Knot Motif*

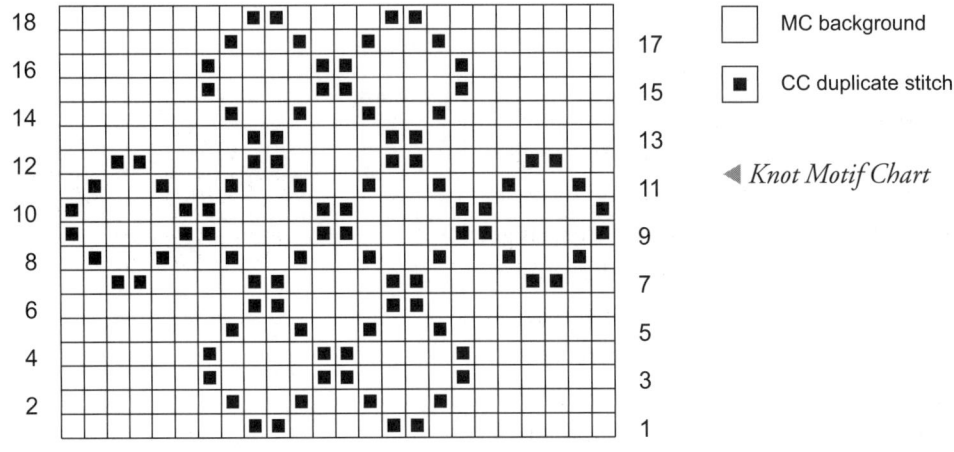

MC background

CC duplicate stitch

◀ *Knot Motif Chart*

Violets Lavender Sachet

As put forth in *Mindful Knitting,* these quick-to-knit gems can express simplicity, ordinary magic, or generosity. Knit them for yourself or as gifts, and fill them with the gifts of the earth— herbs and flax—and infuse them with scented essential oils. A sachet is a beautiful item to place on a bed as good luck charm, as a welcoming baby gift, or to invite a peaceful night's sleep. This take on the basic sachet form, a rectangle with a drawstring, can be embellished or personalized as you like.

▲ *See page 101*

Finished Size: About 4" (10 cm) wide and 6" (15 cm) high.

Yarn: Crystal Palace Mikado Ribbon (50% cotton, 50% rayon; 112 yards [102 meters]/ 50 grams): 1 skein. Shown in #7303 Violets.

Needles: US 7 (4.5 mm) double-pointed needles (dpn), or size to give gauge.

Notions: Measuring tape, yarn needle, scissors, stitch marker, sharp-pointed hand sewing needle, matching sewing thread, ½ yard (0.5 meters) ⅜" (1-cm) satin ribbon, ¼-yard (0.25 meters) sheer material (silk, voile, light cotton) for sachet insert, 1 cup (250 ml) dried lavender flowers, ¼-cup (60 ml) whole flax seed, lavender essential oil (optional), embellishments as desired (ribbon roses, buttons, charms, etc.). Lavender flowers, flax seed (or dried herb of choice, see "personalized scents" sidebar on page 74), and essential oil available in bulk section of many large natural food stores.

Gauge: About 20 sts and 32 rows = 4" (10 cm) in St St worked in the round (rnd). Check your gauge before you begin.

Stitches Used:
Stockinette Stitch (St St) Worked in the Round (Rnd): Knit all sts every rnd.

Techniques Used:
Picot Bind Off: BO 2 sts—1 st on RH needle. *Turn work, and using the knitted method CO 2 more sts. Turn work again—needle with 1 st and 2 new CO sts is RH needle. Pass

personalized scents

Sachets make delightful little gifts for our loved ones, and are an uplifting way to enjoy some of the earth's sweet and restorative bounty. Some common and easy-to-find herbs to consider using in your sachets are:

- Lavender: The aroma-therapeutic and healing qualities of lavender are many. Lavender scent calms and soothes. Lavender possesses anti-depressant properties and is helpful in aiding in relaxation and sleep. This soothing herb helps to freshens rooms, minds, and spirits.

- Rosemary: The woody, evergreen essence of rosemary has long been thought to improve memory. It is often referred to as the herb of "remembrance" and is associated with love and marriage. Traditionally brides, including yours truly, have carried or worn sprigs of rosemary on their wedding day. Rosemary helps overcome mental fatigue, stress, and aids in emotional balance. It is associated with the heart and wisdom.

- Eucalyptus: Eucalyptus is refreshing, bringing brightness to body and mind. It is an immune system booster and possesses antibacterial qualities. It also increases the oxygen in the blood, allowing nutrients to be delivered with more efficiency. Its scent energizes, restores balance, and improves concentration.

- Chamomile: Chamomile calms and comforts. Its scent possesses a slight sedative effect and is helpful in times of stress, anxiety, and irritability. It is considered to have a nurturing quality and is connected with the expression and acceptance of compassion.

- Rose: The romantic scent of rose—a flower immortalized by poets and painters. Rose is associated with the heart, romance, and deep affection. Its scent elevates the spirit and, as an aphrodisiac, encourages love. It can alleviate feelings of sadness and encourage the fading of emotional obstacles.

the second st on RH needle over the first st to BO, then pass the third st on RH needle over the first st to BO—1 st rem on RH needle again. BO the next 2 sts—1 st on RH needle. Rep from * until all sts have been bound off.

Knitted Cast On Method: *Insert RH needle tip into last st on LH needle as if to knit, draw up a loop, then sl the loop to the LH needle to add 1 st. Rep from * to CO the required number of sts, always knitting into the st closest to the tip of the LH needle.

Instructions

Sachet: Loosely CO 40 st onto one dpn. Divide sts as evenly as possible on 3 needles. Join for working in the rnd, being careful not to twist sts, and place marker to indicate beg of rnd. Work even in St St until piece meas 5½" (14 cm) from CO. Work eyelet rnd to create holes for drawstring as foll: *K3, k2tog, yo; rep from * around. Work even in St St until piece meas 5¾" (14.5 cm) from CO. BO all sts using Picot Bind Off.

Sachet insert: Cut two pieces of fabric, each about 3½" x 5½" (11.5 x 14 cm). Place pieces tog with right sides touching, and sew around 3 sides with a ¼" (6-mm) seam allowance, leaving one side open at top (see illustration 1).

Turn insert right side out. Fill with desired contents (see illustration 2), and slipstitch top of insert closed (see illustration 3).

Finishing: Turn sachet inside out and fold so that picots on front and back layers are aligned. With right sides touching, use yarn threaded on a yarn needle to sew bottom seam. Weave in ends. Turn sachet right side out, and apply any additional embellishments. Place sachet insert inside. Thread ribbon through eyelet holes, beg and ending at center front. Draw ribbon tight and tie in a bow.

▲ *Illustration 3*

▲ *Illustration 2*

▲ *Illustration 1*

part three

KNITTER

Through the work of our hands, we discover the basic goodness inherent in all things.
By simply being, we unleash the magic that exists within each moment.

Padma Jacket

In Tantric Buddhism, energy is described as having five basic qualities. They are called the Buddha Families: Vajra, Ratna, Padma, Karma, and Buddha. Each family is associated with an emotion and its corresponding wisdom quality, as well as a color. The emotion of Padma is passion. Its color is red; its transformed wisdom quality is Discriminating Awareness. This wisdom quality is that of seeing precisely and sharply. Where the energy of fiery passion may make us blinded and attached to or lost in a seductive situation, Discriminating Awareness allows the fire to cast light on the importance of the separate elements involved in creating the whole, allowing the passion to inspire rather than blind us.

This Asian-inspired, fitted, rich red "robe" includes seductive elements of color and mixed fibers. Its ornamentation is a swish of flame-like color. As the intarsia design flows around from front to back or side to side, you are invited to work on your own understanding of the dualistic nature of energy and of mind. As you knit through this intarsia piece, you can complete the journey through the transformation of the essence of energy and its impact on your mind and physical being.

This sweater is worked in three pieces, with the front and back of the kimono-style sleeves

knit as part of the body. The fronts and back are sewn together along the top of each sleeve and along the sleeve/side seams. A unique closure—two tabs attached to the front band by beautiful hand blown glass buttons—adds the perfect finishing touch.

◀ *See page 102*

FINISHED SIZE: To fit up to size 40–42
Chest measurement at underarm: 44";
(112 cm)
Total length from lower edge to shoulders:
29"; (73.5 cm)
Sleeve length: 19"; (48.5 cm)
Note: Chest measurement is with fronts
hanging straight down, with edges of front
band just barely touching; for a larger finished chest, instructions are given below for
making longer button tabs so you can wear
the coat with a slight gap down the front, as
desired. Directions for customizing sleeve
length are also given in the instructions
below.

YARN: Mission Falls 1824 Wool (100%
wool; 85 yards [78 meters]/50 grams): 17
skeins main color (MC). Shown in #011
Poppy.

Colinette Prism (70% wool, 30% cotton;
125 yards [114 meters]/100 grams): 5 skeins
contrast color (CC). Shown in #71 Fire.

NEEDLES: US 6 (4 mm) and 8 (5 mm) 29"
(75-cm) circular (circ), or size to give gauge.

NOTIONS: Four ½" (1.3 cm) buttons, measuring tape, yarn needle, scissors, removable
stitch markers or safety pins. Buttons shown:
glass buttons from Moving Mud.

GAUGE: 18 sts and 24 rows = 4" (10 cm) in
St St using Mission Falls 1824 Wool and
larger needle; 16 sts and 24 rows = 4" (10 cm)
in St St using Colinette Prism and larger needle. Check your gauge before you begin.

STITCHES USED:
Stockinette Stitch (St St): Knit all sts on RS
rows, and purl all sts on WS rows.
Seed Stitch
Row 1: (RS) *K1, p1; rep from *, ending k1 if
there is an odd number of sts.
All Other Rows: Purl the knit sts, and knit the
purl sts as they appear to you.

NOTES: Work flame motif in CC in stockinette stitch intarsia, using a different ball of
yarn for each color section, and twisting the
yarns at each color change to avoid leaving a
hole.

The diagrams on pages 85 and 86 show the
approximate placement of the intarsia flame
motif on each garment piece. The pieces have
been marked with dotted lines 1" (2.5 cm)
apart, so each square of the grid represents an
area about 4¼ stitches wide and 6 rows high.
The center of the back is shown with slightly

darker dotted line, and the back left sleeve is not shown to save space.

We encourage you to work the flame motif intuitively, loosely following its path according to the diagram by eyeballing it. If desired, you may check the progress of your flame motif every few inches by measuring. If necessary, adjust the position over the next several inches to bring the flame into agreement with the diagram again. Avoid abrupt angular changes, and try for an easy, naturally-flowing organic outline for the flame.

If you want the flames to meet exactly at the left side seam and right shoulder seam, make sure that the motif meets these edges at the positions shown on the diagram. Otherwise, work as your intuition leads you!

Instructions

Back: With MC and larger needle, CO 112 sts. Work 1 RS row in St St. Cont in St St, CO 2 sts at end of next 4 rows—120 sts. Work even in St St for 9 more rows, ending with a WS row—piece meas about 2½" (6.5 cm) from original CO edge.

Begin flame motif and shape sides: The flame motif is introduced at the same time as the side shaping begins; please read the next section all the way through before proceeding.

Begin working flame motif with CC in St St intarsia on the next RS row as shown on diagram (see Notes). At the same time, beg on the same row as first row of flame motif, shape sides by dec 1 st each end of needle every 6th row 13 times—94 sts; piece meas about 15½" (39.5 cm) from original CO edge when side shaping has been completed. Cont in St St, working flame motif as established, until piece meas 17" (43 cm) from original CO edge, ending with a WS row.

Shape sleeves: Cont in St St and flame motif, inc 1 st at each end of needle every row 10 times—114 sts. At end of next 2 rows, CO 63 sts—240 sts. *Note:* To lengthen or shorten sleeves, CO 1 st more or less for every ¼" (6 mm) of change; adding or removing 4 sts will increase or decrease sleeve length by 1" (2.5 cm). If you customize your sleeve length, keep track of the number of sts changed so you can make the front sleeves the same. Cont even in St St and flame motif until piece meas 7¼" (18.5 cm) from last sleeve CO row, or about 25¾" (65.5 cm) from original CO edge, ending with a WS row.

Shape shoulders and back neck: Cont flame motif, BO 24 sts at beg of next 4 rows—144 sts. If you have customized the sleeves, adjust the number of sts BO so that 144 sts rem.

Mark center 46 sts for back neck with removable markers or safety pins. On next RS row, BO 24 sts, work to marked center sts, join second ball of yarn, BO center 46 sts for back neck, work to end. Working each side separately, on the foll WS row BO 24 sts at beg of first section, work even across second section—25 sts at each side. Working each side separately, and cont flame motif on right back shoulder, work even until piece meas 8½" (21.5 cm) from last sleeve CO row, or about 27" (68.5 cm) from original CO edge. BO all sts loosely.

Right front: With MC and larger needle, CO 51 sts. Work 1 RS row in St St. Cont in St St, CO 2 sts at end of next 2 RS rows—55 sts. Work even in St St until you have completed 14 rows from beg, ending with a WS row—piece meas about 2½" (6.5 cm) from original CO edge.

Begin flame motif and shape side: The flame motif is introduced near the end of the side shaping; please read the next section all the way through before proceeding. Beg on the next RS row, shape side by dec 1 st at side edge (end of RS rows) every 6th row 13 times—42 sts; piece meas about 15½" (39.5 cm) from original CO edge when side shaping has been completed. At the same

time, begin working flame motif with CC in St St intarsia when piece meas about 12" (30.5 cm) from original CO edge, as shown on diagram. Cont in St St, working flame motif as established, until piece meas 17" (43 cm) from original CO edge, ending with a WS row.

Shape right sleeve and right front neck: Cont in St St and flame motif, inc 1 st at side edge (end of RS rows) every row 4 times—46 sts. *Note:* Sleeve and front neck shaping take place at the same time; please read the next section all the way through before proceeding. Cont in St St and flame motif, inc 1 st at side edge every row 6 more times, then CO 63 sts at end of next RS row, or same number of sts CO for back if customizing sleeve length. At the same time, beg on the same row as 5th side increase, dec 1 st at neck edge (beg of RS rows, end of WS rows) every 3 rows 18 times—97 sts when all sleeve and neck shaping has been completed. Cont even in St St and flame motif until piece meas 7¼" (18.5 cm) from last sleeve CO row, or about 25¾" (65.5 cm) from original CO edge, ending with a RS row.

Shape right shoulder: Cont in St St and flame motif, BO 24 sts at beg of next 3 WS rows—25 sts rem. If you have customized the sleeves, adjust the number of sts BO so that 25 sts rem. BO all sts loosely.

Left front: With MC and larger needle, CO 51 sts. Work 1 RS row in St St. Cont in St St, CO 2 sts at end of next 2 WS rows—55 sts. Begin flame motif on next RS row. Work even in St St and flame motif until you have completed 14 rows from beg, ending with a WS row—piece meas about 2½" (6.5 cm) from original CO edge.

Shape side: Cont in St St and flame motif, beg on next RS row, by dec 1 st at side edge (beg of RS rows) every 6th row 13 times—42 sts; piece meas about 15½" (39.5 cm) from original CO edge when side shaping has been completed. Cont in St St, working flame motif as established, until piece meas 17" (43 cm) from original CO edge, ending with a WS row.

Shape left sleeve and left front neck: Cont in St St, inc 1 st at side edge (beg of RS rows) every row 4 times—46 sts. *Note:* Sleeve and front neck shaping take place at the same time; please read the next section all the way through before proceeding. Cont in St St, inc 1 st at side edge every row 6 more times, then CO 63 sts at end of next WS row, or same number of sts CO for back if customizing

sleeve length. At the same time, beg on the same row as 5th side increase, dec 1 st at neck edge (end of RS rows, beg of WS rows) every 3 rows 18 times—97 sts when all sleeve and neck shaping has been completed. Cont even in St St and flame motif until piece meas 7¼" (18.5 cm) from last sleeve CO row, or about 25¾" (65.5 cm) from original CO edge, ending with a WS row.

Shape left shoulder: Cont in St St, BO 24 sts at beg of next 3 RS rows—25 sts rem. If you have customized the sleeves, adjust the number of sts BO so that 25 sts rem. BO all sts loosely.

Bottom bands: With CC, RS facing and smaller needles, pick up and knit 125 sts evenly along shaped lower edge of back, from selvedge to selvedge. Work in Seed St for 2" (5 cm). BO all sts loosely. With CC, RS facing and smaller needle, pick up and knit 57 sts evenly along shaped lower edge of right front, from selvedge to selvedge. Work in Seed St for 2" (5 cm). BO all sts loosely. Work lower edge of left front same as for right front.

Front band: With yarn needle and matching yarn to the sts being joined, sew fronts and back together at shoulders. With CC, RS facing and smaller needle, beg at lower edge of right front bottom band, pick up and knit 117 sts along right front edge to shoulder, 2 sts at right side of back neck, 44 sts across back neck, 2 sts at left side of back neck, and 117 sts along left front edge from shoulder to lower edge of left front bottom band—282 sts. Work even in Seed St until front band meas 2" (5 cm) from pickup row. BO all sts loosely as if to knit.

Sleeve bands: With CC, RS facing and smaller needle, pick up and knit 72 sts evenly along cuff edge of sleeve. Work in Seed St for 2" (5 cm). BO all sts loosely. Work second sleeve band the same as the first.

Button tabs: With CC and smaller needle, CO 14 sts. *Note:* To increase finished chest measurement by making longer button tabs, CO 1 more st for every additional ¼" (6 mm), or 4 sts for every extra 1" (2.5 cm) desired. Work in Seed St for 4 rows. On the next row, work buttonholes as foll: Work 2 sts in patt, BO 2 sts, work in patt to last 4 sts, BO 2 sts, work 2 sts in patt. On the foll row, CO 2 sts above each gap in the previous row to complete buttonholes. Work 4 more rows Seed St. BO all sts. Make second button tab same as the first.

Finishing: With yarn needle and matching yarn to the sts being joined, sew sleeve and side seams, leaving sides of seed st lower bands open for 2" (5 cm) slits at each side. Weave in ends. Try on coat and mark position for best placement of button tab closures. For the coat shown, the lower set of buttons is 12" (30.5 cm) up from lower edge, and the higher set is 18" (45.5 cm) up from lower edge, about 2" (5 cm) below beg of neck shaping. Sew buttons at marked positions centered on front band.

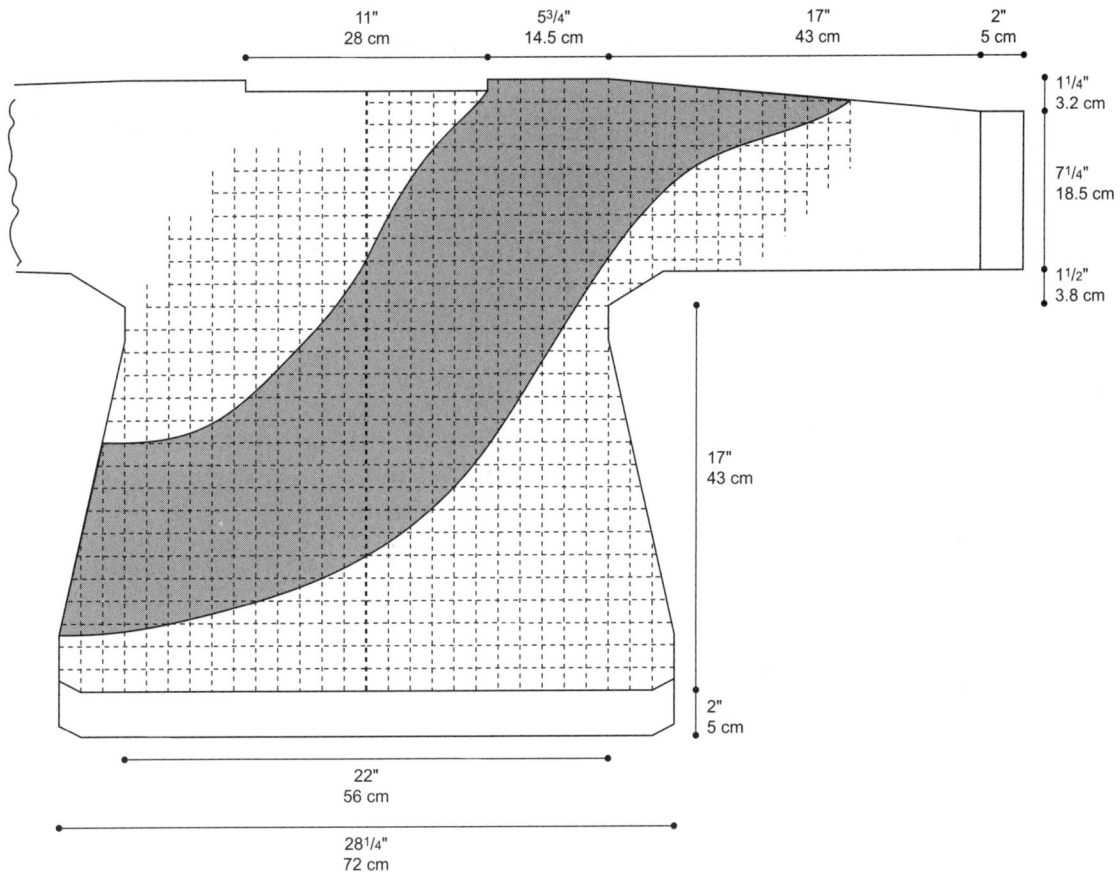

11"
28 cm

5³/4"
14.5 cm

17"
43 cm

2"
5 cm

1¹/4"
3.2 cm

7¹/4"
18.5 cm

1¹/2"
3.8 cm

17"
43 cm

2"
5 cm

22"
56 cm

28¹/4"
72 cm

▲ *Padma Jacket, Back*

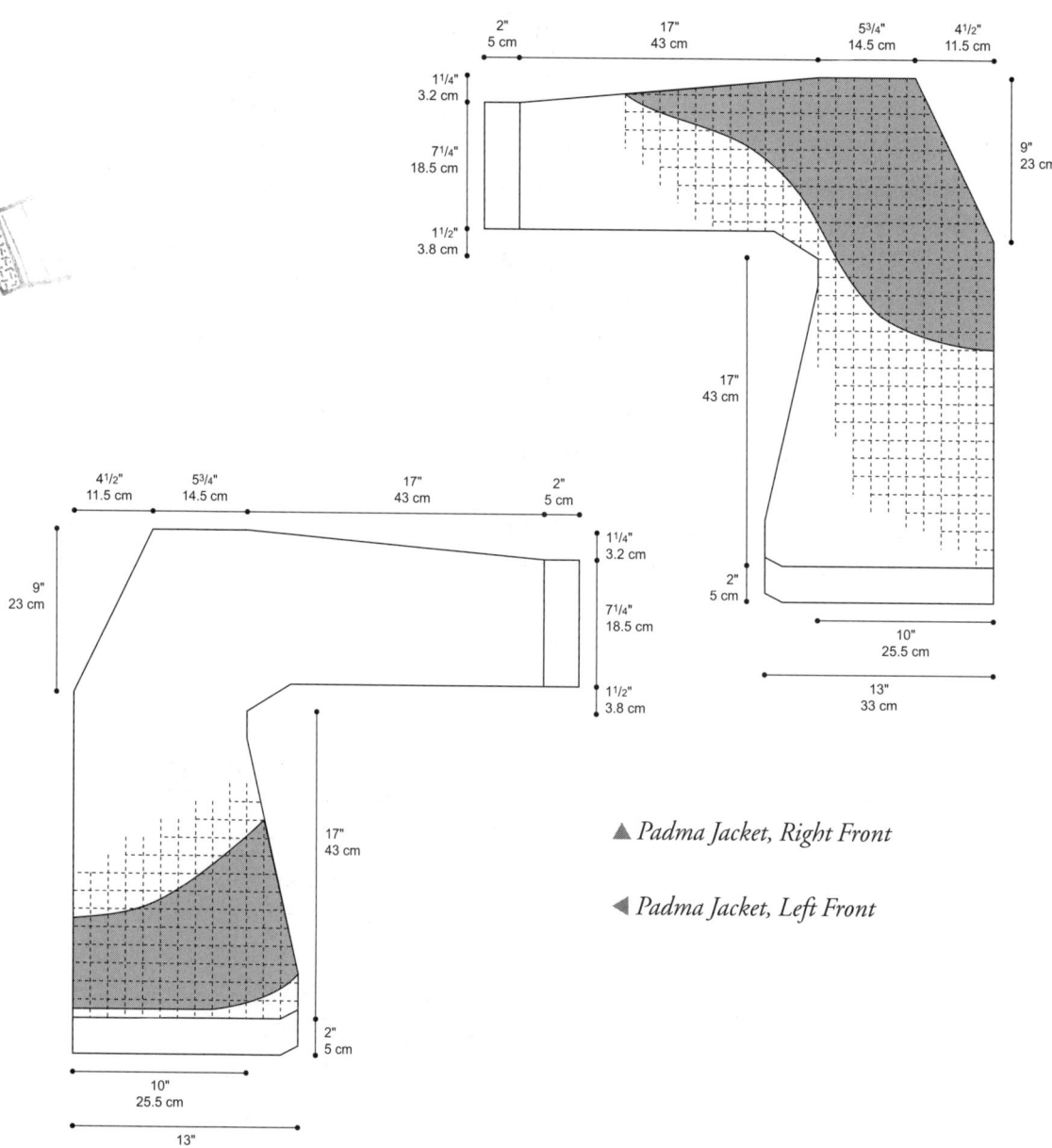

▲ *Padma Jacket, Right Front*

◀ *Padma Jacket, Left Front*

AUSPICIOUS COINCIDENCES BABY SWEATER

This sweater is an exercise in self discipline, creativity, and yarn stash reduction. This "make it up as you go" sweater will give the mindful knitter a basic framework in which to create a beautiful one-of-a-kind baby sweater. The rules of the game are simple: stick your hand in your yarn basket and work with whatever it finds there—no ifs, ands, or buts. The discipline of working through something even if you don't like it is much like the meditator's path: it reminds you to stay present and persevere through a challenging situation.

The body is worked in one piece to the underarms. The upper back, upper fronts, and sleeves are all worked separately, allowing the knitter to work with the notion of coincidence, and *wabi sabi* (see page 88). Plus, there's the added benefit of stash reduction, lightening our fiber load—or making way for new wealth. The finished sweater will appear to have the same basic colorway overall, and will be further unified by the color you select for your trim. Have faith, keep knitting, you will be very pleasantly surprised when you are done!

FINISHED SIZE: To fit 6–12 months (12–18 months, 18–24 months); shown in size 12–18 months
Chest measurement: 22 (24, 28)"; (56 [61, 71] cm)
Total length: 11 (13, 15)"; (28 [33, 38] cm)
Sleeve length: 7½ (8½, 10)"; (19 [21.5, 25.5] cm)

See page 104 ▶

wabi sabi—the beauty of imperfection

Within the Japanese view of esthetics, we find the notion of wabi sabi. Wabi, which roughly means *things that are simple*, and Sabi, *things that have gained beauty and dignity with use and age*, is an appreciation, acceptance, and celebration of the beauty of imperfection, impermanence, and the incomplete. Within the philosophy of wabi sabi, we find a celebration of the humble and ordinary. Wabi sabi relates with the raw and unpretentious beauty of the natural world. This notion of the exploration of beauty invites the viewer to investigate and discover for themselves the hidden magic and unrevealed majesty to be found in a piece of art, a gesture, a tree, and in life.

YARN: Approximately 7 (9, 12) ounces (200 [250, 325] grams) of random stash yarn from DK to worsted weight with an average gauge of about 20 sts per 4" (10 cm).

NEEDLES: US 5 (3.75 mm) straight, and two sets of US 7 (4.5 mm) straight, or size to give gauge on larger needles.

NOTIONS: Six assorted ½" (1.3-cm) buttons, measuring tape, yarn needle, scissors, stitch holders, crochet hook size J/10 (6 mm; optional), eight 3" x 5" (7.5 x 12 cm) index cards.

GAUGE: 20 sts and 28 rows = 4" (10 cm) in St St for most of the yarns selected using larger needles. Check your gauge before you begin.

STITCHES USED:
Seed Stitch (worked over an even number of sts)
Row 1: *K1, p1; rep from * to end.
Row 2: *P1, k1; rep from * to end.
Rep these 2 rows for patt.

TECHNIQUES USED: Two-Row, Two-Stitch Buttonhole, Three-Needle Bind-Off Technique (see page 19 for both).

NOTES: The cardigan is knit in one piece to the underarms, then divided into the back and two fronts that are worked separately to the shoulders.

If you prefer matching fronts (although this is not recommended), work the first one randomly according to the Auspicious Knitting guidelines below, and take notes about the sequence of stripes and colors you use. The same goes for making matching sleeves.

You might wish to knit in or weave in the ends as you go in order to minimize the number of ends to be woven in when finishing the sweater.

Guidelines for Auspicious Knitting

Choose yarns: Select a pile of yarns from your stash that will knit to an average gauge of about 5 sts and 7 rows to the inch (20 sts and 28 rows to 10 cm). This means that a wide range of weights and textures is fair game, from DK to worsted with the occasional bulky yarn thrown in, too. Choose colors that harmonize well with each other. Amounts can range from full balls to little scraps that are just long enough to work one row.

Choose a trim color: There should be enough of this color to use it throughout the sweater and still have enough to left over to work the Seed Stitch trim for the lower edge, neck and front bands, and sleeve cuffs—perhaps one or two balls. The trim color will pull the whole project together, unifying all the assorted colors into a harmonious whole. Place all your chosen yarns in a basket or big bag.

Prepare the stripe sequences: On the index cards, write each of the following four stripe sequences. There are four sequences and eight cards, so you will write each sequence on two separate cards. Colors are indicated by the letter C followed by a number: C1, C2, and so forth.

Sequence One (3 colors, 6 rows)
Rows 1–2: Knit with C1.
Rows 3–4: Knit with C2.
Rows 5–6: Knit with C3.

Sequence Two (2 colors, 6 rows)
Row 1: Knit with C1.
Row 2: Purl with C1.
Rows 3–4: Knit with C2.
Row 5: Knit with C1.
Row 6: Purl with C1.

Sequence Three (4 colors, 4 rows)
Row 1: Knit with C1.
Row 2: Purl with C2.
Row 3: Knit with C3.
Row 4: Purl with C4.

Sequence Four (4 colors, 6 rows)

Row 1: Knit with C1.

Row 2: Purl with C2.

Row 3: Knit with C3.

Row 4: *K1, p1; rep from * across with C4.

Row 5: Knit with C2.

Row 6: Purl with C1.

Using the stripe sequences: The basic instructions for the sweater are given below. After knitting the Seed Stitch trim at the lower edge, begin your auspicious knitting. Shuffle the index cards and pick one at random. Next, reach into your stash basket and blindly select the number of colors needed for the sequence shown on the card, designating them as C1, C2, C3, or C4 in the order you pick them. Work the rows in the colors indicated on the card. When you finish the rows on one card, re-shuffle and pick another card, then reach back into the stash for the next group of colors. If you happen to pick the same stripe sequence card again, that's great. You will probably have selected a different group of random colors for it, which will be very exciting!

As you continue to work in pattern from the stripe sequence cards, don't forget to follow the shaping directions according to the basic sweater instructions. Resist the temptation to swap one color for another, or rip out stripes because you don't like them. As in all things, if you take a step back and regard a small section as a part of a greater whole, you will see that it blends nicely into the entirety.

Instructions

Lower body: With trim color and smaller needles, CO 110 (120, 140) sts. Work in Seed St for 1" (2.5 cm), ending with a RS row. Purl across the next WS row with trim color. Change to larger needles, and begin working in stripe sequences with random colors as given above. Work even until piece meas 6 (7, 8)" (15 [18, 20.5] cm) from CO edge, ending with a WS row.

Divide for back and fronts: On next RS row, work 26 (28, 34) sts, place the sts just worked on spare larger straight needle for right front, BO 2 sts for armhole, work 54 (60, 68) sts for back, BO 2 sts for armhole, work rem 26 (28, 34) sts to end of row, and place the last group of sts on spare larger straight needle for left front.

Back: Rejoin yarn to 54 (60, 68) sts of back with WS facing. Cont in stripe sequences with random colors until armholes meas 4½ (5½, 6½)" (11.5 [14, 16.5] cm), ending with a WS row.

Back neck shaping: On next RS row, work 16 (18, 20) sts in patt, join ball of same color and BO center 22 (24, 28) sts for back neck, work to end—16 (18, 20) sts at each side for shoulder. Working each side separately, cont in patt until armholes meas 5 (6, 7)" (12.5 [15, 18] cm), and piece meas about 11 (13, 15)" (28 [33, 38] cm) from CO edge. Place 16 (18, 20) sts for each shoulder on separate holders.

Right front: Rejoin yarn to 26 (28, 34) sts of right front with WS facing. Cont in stripe sequences with random colors until armhole meas 2½ (3½, 4½)" (6.5 [9, 11.5] cm), ending with a WS row.

Right front neck shaping: On next RS row, BO 6 (6, 8) sts, work to end—20 (22, 26) sts. Dec 1 st at neck edge every RS row 4 (4, 6) times—16 (18, 20) sts rem. Cont in patt until armhole meas 5 (6, 7)" (12.5 [15, 18] cm), and piece meas about 11 (13, 15)" (28 [33, 38] cm) from CO edge. Place 16 (18, 20) sts for shoulder on holder.

Left front: Rejoin yarn to 26 (28, 34) sts of left front with WS facing. Work as for right front, reversing neck shaping by binding off at beg of a WS row. Copy the same stripe sequences and colors, or go totally random. (Be brave!) Place 16 (18, 20) sts for shoulder on holder.

Shoulder joining: Using three-needle bind-off technique (see page 19), join shoulders together, right sides facing, carefully matching left front to left back and right front to right back. The side of the garment with the three-needle bind-off ridge is the WS of the garment.

Sleeves: The sleeves are worked from the top edge down to the cuff. With larger needles, CO 50 (60, 70) sts. Cont in stripe sequences with random colors, and at the same time, shape sleeves by dec 1 st each end of needle every 4 rows 9 (12, 15) times—32 (36, 40) sts. Work even until sleeve meas 6½ (7½, 9)" (16.5 [19, 23] cm) from CO edge, ending with a WS row. Change to trim color and smaller needles, and knit 1 RS row. Work in Seed St for 1" (2.5 cm)—piece meas about 7½ (8½, 10)" (19 [21.5, 25.5] cm) from CO edge. BO all sts.

Make a second sleeve the same as the first, working randomly or using the same stripe sequences and colors as you prefer.

Neckband: With smaller needles and trim color, using crochet hook to assist if desired, with RS facing pick up and knit 48 (50, 56) sts evenly around neck opening. Work in Seed St for 1" (2.5) cm. Loosely BO all sts.

Buttonband: (worked on left front for girls, right front for boys or a unisex garment) With smaller needles and trim color, using crochet hook to assist if desired, with RS facing pick up and knit 42 (52, 62) sts evenly along center front opening. Work in Seed St for 6 rows. Loosely BO all sts.

Buttonhole band: (worked on right front for girls, left front for boys or a unisex garment) With smaller needles and trim color, using crochet hook to assist if desired, with RS facing pick up and knit 42 (52, 62) sts evenly along center front opening. Work in Seed St for 2 rows. On the next 2 rows, make six buttonholes using the two-row, two-stitch buttonhole method, with the lowest buttonhole ½" (1.3 cm) up from CO edge, the highest ½" (1.3 cm) down from top edge of neckband, and the rem 4 buttonholes about 1½ (2, 2¼)" (3.8 [5, 5.5] cm) apart. (See Tip for More Intuitive Knitting: Buttonhole Placement on page 93.) Work 2 more rows Seed St. Loosely BO all sts.

Sew sleeves into armholes. Sew sleeve seams. Weave in ends. Securely sew 6 buttons to front buttonband, corresponding with buttonhole positions. Steam block lightly, if needed, to even out the appearance of the various yarns.

washing instructions

When combining many different types of yarn, always wash according to the instructions for the most delicate. For example, if you are mixing machine-washable wool with fine kid mohair, wash the garment by hand according to the care instructions for the mohair.

tip for more intuitive knitting: buttonhole placement

Knit the band or garment front that will not have buttonholes first, then mark the button locations with safety pins, either by measuring or eyeballing it. When you make the band or garment front that has buttonholes, compare it to the band with the safety pin markers. When you reach the approximate location of each pin, it's time to make a buttonhole. Continue in this manner until all the buttonholes have been completed.

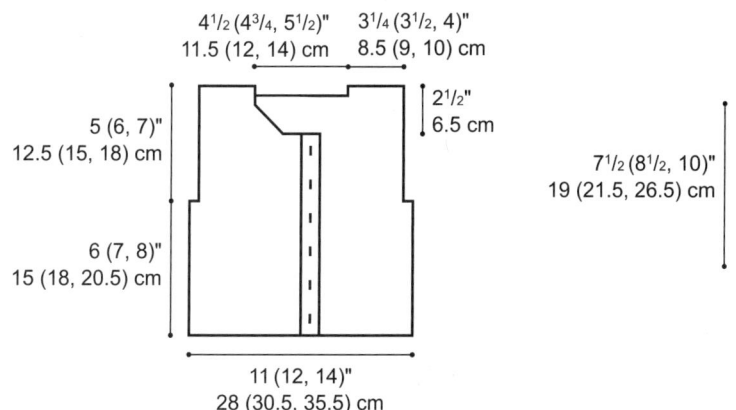
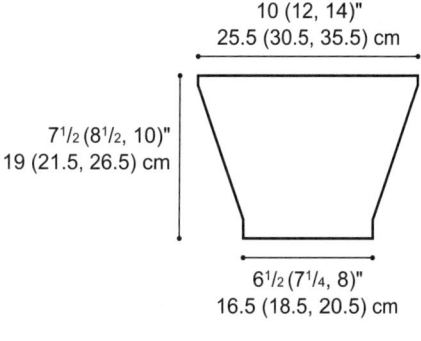

▲ *Auspicious Coincidences Baby Sweater*

Spring Toque
for Babies and Kids and Grownups

The first signs of springs bring the excitement of fresh bright colors after a long winter. This special hat combines soft wool and cotton chenille and is perfect to wear on those early spring days when the air is still chilly, or during the winter to brighten up our senses and remind us that spring is on the way. This toque style hat with its playful topknot is a quick, fun project that combines textural interest with a simple two-color knitting technique. It makes a wonderful learning project, and a wonderful gift.

Finished Size: To fit infant (toddler, child, adult); shown in toddler's size
Head circumference: 16 (17, 19, 21)"; 40.5 (43, 48.5, 53.5) cm
Height from cast-on edge to beginning of crown shaping: 4½ (5¼, 6, 7)"; (11.5 [13.5, 15, 18] cm)

Yarn: Crystal Palace Iceland (100% wool; 109 yards [100 meters]/100 grams): 1 skein main color (MC). Shown in #7245 Seafoam. Crystal Palace Cotton Chenille (100% cotton; 98 yards [90 meters]/50 grams): 1 skein each of 2 colors used doubled. Shown in #2214 Brite Blue (CC1) and #2342 Spring Green (CC2).

Needles: US 9 (5.5 mm) 16" (40 cm) circular (circ) and double-pointed needles (dpn), or size to give gauge.

Notions: Measuring tape, yarn needle, scissors, stitch marker.

Gauge: 16 sts and 22 rows = 4" (10 cm) in St St worked in the round (rnd) using MC. Check your gauge before you begin.

Stitches Used:
Stockinette Stitch (St St) Worked in the Round (Rnd): Knit all sts every rnd.

◀ *See page 104*

Instructions

Lower border: With double strand of CC1 and circ needle, loosely CO 64 (68, 76, 84) sts. Join for working in the rnd, being careful not to twist sts, and place marker (pm) to indicate beg of rnd. Work 7 rnds as foll:

Rnds 1 and 2: With CC1, purl 2 rnds.

Rnds 3 and 4: With MC, knit 2 rnds.

Rnds 5, 6, and 7: With double strand of CC2, knit 1 rnd, then purl 2 rnds.

Change to double strand of MC and knit 2 (4, 6, 9) rnds—piece meas about 1½ (2, 2¼, 3)" (3.8 [5, 5.5, 7.5] cm) from CO edge.

Checkerboard patt: Work next 8 rnds as foll:

Rnds 1 and 2: With double strand of CC1, knit 2 rnds.

Rnds 3 and 4: *K2 with double strand of CC1, k2 with CC2; rep from * to end.

Rnds 5 and 6: *K2 with double strand of CC2, k2 with CC1; rep from * to end.

Rnds 7 and 8: With double strand of CC1, knit 2 rnds.

Upper border: Change to double strand of MC and knit 2 (4, 6, 9) rnds. Work 8 rnds as foll:

Rnds 1, 2, and 3: With double strand of CC1, knit 1 rnd, then purl 2 rnds.

Rnds 4 and 5: With double strand of MC, knit 2 rnds.

Rnds 6, 7, and 8: With double strand of CC2, knit 1 rnd, then purl 2 rnds—piece meas about 4½ (5¼, 6, 7)" (11.5 [13.5, 15, 18] cm) from CO edge.

Shape crown: Cut CC1 and CC2, leaving 8" (20-cm) tails to be woven in later. With MC, knit 1 rnd, dec 1 (inc 2, inc 1, inc 0) sts—63 (70, 77, 84) sts. Dec for top of crown as foll, changing to dpn when there are too few sts to fit comfortably around circ needle:

Rnd 1: *K7 (8, 9, 10), k2tog; rep from * to end—56 (63, 70, 77) sts.

All Even-Numbered Rnds: Knit.

Rnd 3: *K6 (7, 8, 9), k2tog; rep from * to end—49 (56, 63, 70) sts.

Rnd 5: *K5 (6, 7, 8), k2tog; rep from * to end—42 (49, 56, 63) sts.

Rnd 7: *K4, (5, 6, 7), k2tog; rep from * to end—35 (42, 49, 56) sts.

Rnd 9: *K3 (4, 5, 6, 7), k2tog; rep from * to end—28 (35, 42, 49) sts.

Rnd 11: *K2 (3, 4, 5), k2tog; rep from * to end—21 (28, 35, 42) sts.

Rnd 13: *K1 (2, 3, 4), k2tog; rep from * to end—14 (21, 28, 35) sts.

Rnd 15: For infant's size only, work k2tog around—7 sts rem; skip to Topknot instructions below. Work 3 rem sizes as *K (1, 2, 3), k2tog; rep from * to end—(14, 21, 28) sts.

Rnd 17: For toddler's size only, work k2tog around—7 sts rem; skip to Topknot instructions below. Work 2 rem sizes as *K (1, 2), k2tog; rep from * to end—(14, 21) sts.

Rnd 19: For child's size only, work k2tog around—7 sts rem; skip to Topknot instructions below. Work rem size as *K1, k2tog; rep from * to end—(14) sts.

Rnd 21: For adult size only, work k2tog around—7 sts rem.

Topknot: Work in St St on rem 7 sts until cord for topknot meas 5" (12.5 cm) from last dec rnd, or desired length. Cut yarn leaving a 12" (30-cm) tail, draw through rem sts, pull snugly to close top of cord, and bring yarn tail to inside of cord.

Finishing: Weave in ends. Tie an overhand knot with topknot cord.

HEAVEN AND STARS BABY SET *see page 18*

CLOUD PILLOW *see page 15*

ANGELS
AND FAIRIES
see page 38

AUTUMN LEAVES BLANKET
see page 26

WISP OF MIST
WRIST WARMERS
see page 29

BLACK SAND HAORI VEST   *see page 65*

TRAVEL ACCESSORIES   *see page 31*

SEA ARAN CARDIGAN *see page 45*

GIFTS OF WARMTH
AND COMPASSION
MITTENS & SCARF *see page 105*

SKY LAKE JACKET *see page 52*

VIOLETS LAVENDER SACHET *see page 105*

PADMA JACKET *see page 79*

FENG SHUI CHARM *see page 108*

SNOWFALL WRAP *see page 63*

WALKING MEDITATION SOCKS

see page 68

AUSPICIOUS COINCIDENCES BABY SWEATER
see page 87

SPRING TOQUE
see page 94

GIFTS OF WARMTH AND COMPASSION
MITTENS AND SCARF

The warmth of the heart, the literal warmth of the body, and the healing quality of heat—such is the essence of these gifts. These mittens and scarf are easy and quick-to-knit items that will come directly from the heart of the giver to warm the heart of the recipient. They serve as a reminder to stay open to opportunities and to explore generosity in all things, all situations, and always within ourselves. The thick, plush wool, unisex color, and simple styling will assure that this gift will be well received by everyone.

COMPASSIONATE MITTENS

FINISHED SIZE: Woman's medium (large); shown in woman's large
Hand circumference: 7½ (8)"; (19 [20.5] cm)
Length from cast-on edge to fingertips with lower edge unrolled: 10½ (11)"; (26.5 [28] cm)

YARN: Crystal Palace Iceland (100% wool; 109 yards [100 meters]/100 grams): 1 skein.

◀ *See page 100*

Shown in #9572 Kelim. Note: You will need 3 skeins to make both mittens and scarf.

NEEDLES: US 10 (6 mm) double-pointed needles (dpn), or size to give gauge.

NOTIONS: Markers, measuring tape, yarn needle, scissors, stitch holders or scrap yarn.

GAUGE: 14 sts and 21 rows = 4" (10 cm) in St St worked in the round (rnd). Check your gauge before you begin.

STITCHES USED:
Stockinette Stitch (St St) Worked in the Round (Rnd): Knit all sts every rnd.

Instructions

Right mitten: Loosely CO 26 (28) sts with MC. Join for working in the rnd, being careful not to twist sts, and place marker (pm) to indicate beg of rnd. Work even in St St until piece meas 6 (6¼)" (15 [16] cm) from CO edge or desired length to thumb opening.

Right thumb opening: K1, place next 5 sts on holder or scrap yarn, CO 5 sts over gap, and cont to end of rnd in St St—still 26 (28) sts.

Hand: Cont even in St St until piece meas 9 (9½)" (23 [24] cm) from CO edge, or about 1½" (3.8 cm) less than desired finished length.

Shape mitten top:
Rnd 1: K2tog, k9 (10), k2tog twice, k9 (10), k2tog—22 (24) sts.
Even-numbered Rnds 2, 4, and 6: Knit.
Rnd 3: K2tog, k7 (8), k2tog twice, k7 (8), k2tog—18 (20) sts.
Rnd 5: K2tog, k5 (6), k2tog twice, k5 (6), k2tog—14 (16) sts.
Rnd 7: K2tog, k3 (4), k2tog twice, k3 (4), k2tog—10 (12) sts.
Cut yarn leaving an 8" (20-cm) tail, draw through rem sts, pull snugly to close top of mitten, and bring yarn tail to inside of mitten.

Thumb: Place 5 sts of thumb opening on one dpn. Join yarn to beg of these sts and knit across them. With a second dpn, pick up and knit 1 st from the side of the opening, 5 sts from the base of the sts cast on for top of opening, and 1 st from other side of opening—12 sts. Distribute sts evenly on 3 needles, and pm for beg of rnd. Knit 1 rnd, dec 1 st for size medium only—11 (12) sts. Work even in St St until thumb meas 2(2¼)" or (5 [5.5] cm) ½" (1.3 cm) less than desired length.

Shape thumb tip:
Rnd 1: *K2tog, k2; rep from * to last 3 (4) sts, end k2tog, k1 (2)—8 (9) sts.
Rnd 2: Knit.
Rnd 3: *K2tog; rep from * to last 2 (3) sts, end k2tog, k0 (1)—4 (5) sts.
Cut yarn leaving an 8" (20-cm) tail, draw through rem sts, pull snugly to close thumb tip, and bring yarn tail to inside of thumb.

Left mitten: Work same as right mitten until piece meas 6 (6¼)" (15 [16] cm) from CO edge or desired length to thumb opening.

Left thumb opening: K7, place next 5 sts on holder or scrap yarn, CO 5 sts over gap, and cont to end of rnd in St St—still 26 (28) sts.

Complete left mitten hand, mitten top, and thumb as for right mitten.

Finishing: Weave in ends. Block lightly if desired; bottom edge will roll naturally to the outside.

WARM SCARF

FINISHED SIZE: 6" (15 cm) wide and 48" long (122 cm) with rib relaxed

YARN: Crystal Palace Iceland (100% wool; 109 yards [100 meters]/100 grams): 2 skeins. Shown in #9572 Kelim. *Note:* You will need 3 skeins to make both mittens and scarf.

NEEDLES: US 11 (8 mm), or size to give gauge.

NOTIONS: Measuring tape, yarn needle, scissors.

GAUGE: 17½ sts and 14 rows = 4" (10 cm) in k2, p2 rib with rib relaxed. Check your gauge before you begin.

STITCHES USED:
K2, P2 Rib (multiple of 4 sts, plus 2)
Row 1: *K2, p2; rep from * to last 2 sts, end k2.

Row 2: *P2, k2; rep from * to last 2 sts, end p2.
Rep these 2 rows for patt.

NOTE: You can keep knitting the scarf until you run out of yarn, but you will need to leave a tail about 10 times the width of the piece for binding off. To check that you have enough yarn left to complete the bind off row, spread the scarf out on the needle as wide as it will comfortably stretch, and wrap the tail loosely around the scarf close to the needle, being careful not to draw in the edges of the scarf. If you can wrap the tail completely around at least 5 times (the same as 10 times the width), then there is enough yarn left to bind off.

Instructions
Loosely CO 26 sts. Work in k2, p2 rib until piece meas 48" (122 cm) from CO edge or until you run out of yarn. Loosely BO all sts in rib patt. Weave in ends.

FENG SHUI CHARM

Feng shui, or the ancient art of geomancy, has gained great popularity recently in the West. For its practitioners and subscribers it has enriched their lives by drawing their awareness to positive and negative energies and how they affect aspects of our outer and inner worlds. This ancient eastern philosophy is based on encouraging the most fortuitous and healthful flow of energy through space, bodies, houses, and lives. In some places it is taken so seriously that homes are often not constructed until the land and the plans have the approval of the geomancer.

▲ *See page 102*

Feng shui charms, or "cures," invite us to work with the existing elements of our lives from a start-where-you-are-now approach. By encouraging the flow of energy in a certain way we can bring attention to a condition or situation or use a desirable element to improve it. Offering a charm invites or reflects energy from a specific location to enhance or invite its positive effects, or to protect us from rushing and negative energy flows. This charm can be filled with special items, like coins or blessings, and placed in key feng shui locations to activate or hinder energy flow.

FINISHED SIZE: About 5" (12.5-cm) square.

YARN: Crystal Palace Mikado Ribbon (50% cotton, 50% rayon; 112 yards [102 meters]/50 grams): 1 skein. Shown in #1797 Jewel Red.

NEEDLES: US 7 (4.5 mm) double-pointed needles (dpn), or size to give gauge.

NOTIONS: Measuring tape, yarn needle, scissors, stitch marker, sharp-pointed hand sewing needle, matching sewing thread, wool roving for stuffing, ⅓ yard (0.3 meters) 1" (2.5-cm) ribbon for hanging, embellishments as desired (ribbon roses, buttons, charms, etc.). Button shown: large red and gold glass button from Moving Mud.

GAUGE: About 20 sts and 32 rows = 4" (10 cm) in St St Worked in the Round (rnd). Check your gauge before you begin.

STITCHES USED:

Stockinette Stitch (St St) Worked in the Round (Rnd): Knit all sts every rnd.

TECHNIQUES USED: Three-Needle Bind-Off Technique (see page 19).

Instructions

Charm: Loosely CO 50 sts onto one dpn. Divide sts as evenly as possible on 3 dpn. Join for working in the rnd, being careful not to twist sts, and place marker to indicate beg of rnd. Work even in St St until piece meas 5" (12.5 cm) from CO. Carefully turn piece inside out with needles in place, and re-arrange sts evenly on 2 needles—25 sts each needle. With right sides facing, use the Three-Needle Bind-Off Technique to close top of charm.

Finishing: Turn charm right side out and embellish as desired (personalized decorative embroidery or accent items). Fill the charm with things that relate to its desired effect: coins for wealth, a crystal for protection, a beautiful button or charm with personal significance, and so on. Add a few rose petals for love and relationships, images of a new job, travel destinations, a poem or special words. Fill the rest of the interior with wool roving or batting to protect the other items. With yarn threaded on a yarn needle, sew bottom seam. Weave in ends. Attach hanging ribbon to upper corners using sewing needle and thread as shown.

Hang the charm in a window or an area of your home or office that requires extra protection or needs its positive qualities activated. See Bibliography and Further Reading on page 131 for suggested books on feng shui and interior environments.

terms and abbreviations

Beg	Beginning	**K1, P1 Rib**	Knit 1, Purl 1 Rib
BO	Bind Off	**K1F&B**	Knit into front and back of same st to increase 1 st
CC	Contrast Color		
Circ	Circular, as in circular needle	**K2tog**	Knit 2 stitches together as one
cm	Centimeter		
CO	Cast On	**LH**	Left Hand
Cont	Continue	**MC**	Main Color
Dec	Decrease	**Meas**	Measures
DPN	Double-Pointed Needle	**mm**	Millimeter
EOR	Every Other Row	**Ndl(s)**	Needle(s)
Foll	Follows, Following	**P**	Purl
Garter St	Garter Stitch	**PSSO**	Pass slipped stitch over
Gauge	The number of stitches across and rows up and down in a certain length. Achieving the specified gauge is essential when knitting a pattern.	**Patt**	Pattern
		PM	Place Marker
		Rem	Remaining
		Rep	Repeat
		Rev St St	Reverse Stockinette Stitch
In	Inch	**RH**	Right Hand
Inc	Increase	**Rnd**	Round
K	Knit	**RS**	Right Side

Sl	Slip		**Tog**	Together
SSK	Slip, Slip, Knit (left-leaning decrease)		**WS**	Wrong Side
			WYIF	With Yarn in Front
St St	Stockinette Stitch		**YO**	Yarnover
St(s)	Stitch(es)			

tips and techniques

Each pattern in this book includes a list of techniques used that may be new or to which you might wish to refer. Please consult the list below to find an explanation of the technique in which you are interested.

Binding Off: The technique used to finish off the edge of a knitted fabric, removing it from the needles. Opposite of Casting On. In English knitting terminology, this is referred to as Casting Off. The most common method of Binding Off is to begin by knitting two stitches, then inserting the tip of the left-hand needle into the first stitch knit and lifting it up and over the second stitch knit, then allowing it to drop off the needle. To complete the action, two stitches are required. Once the first stitch is Bound Off, one stitch remains on the right-hand needle. Knit another stitch from the left-hand needle, again giving you two stitches, and repeat the process. If you ever have more than two stitches on the right-hand needle, you have not successfully completed a Bind Off, and need to go back and redo the process with two stitches.

Blocking: Process to even out the tension of stitches and to flatten rolling edges of a knit fabric. Blocking can be done using a steam iron on cool setting, or by washing a garment, shaping it to the desired shape and pinning it in place to dry. Patterned stitches should be blocked *only if absolutely necessary.* Blocking flattens knit stitches and compromises the desired textured effect.

Buttonholes: See Two-Row Two Stitch Buttonhole (page 19), A Note on Buttonholes (page 19), and Intuitive Knitting Tip: Buttonhole Placement (page 93).

Casting On: The technique of putting stitches on the needles to begin knitting a piece of fabric. Many methods of casting on exist, each giving a unique quality or edge finish. A pattern may call for a particular cast-on to achieve a desired effect or elasticity. Consult a knitting reference book for more information and instructions on the various types of Casting On. The technique recommended for the projects in this book, and for general use, is the Two-Tail Cast-On, also known as the Long Tail or Double Cast-On.

> **Two-Tail Cast-On**—One of the most common methods of casting on, this method gives a sturdy and neat edge to your work. If you do not know how to complete a Two-Tail Cast-On, please consult an illustrated knitting reference for instruction. Some tips for Casting On using this method: To measure out a length of yarn for the "tail," a good rule is to measure approximately 1 inch for each stitch you plan to cast on. Then, at the point where you have reached that length, make a slip knot. Place the slipknot on one of the knitting needles and secure it in place. It should be loose enough to slide back and forth but tight enough to stay on the needle if you shake it.

Circular Needles (Circular Knitting): Two short needles attached together by a cord, typically made from plastic. The needles themselves may be made of a variety of materials—aluminum, plastic, wood, or bamboo. Circular needles come in a variety of lengths, most commonly 16, 24, and 29 inches. If you are using them to knit in the round (see below), you should choose a needle with a length that is slightly less than the circumference of your work.

> **Knitting in the Round with Circular Needles**—The main purpose of circular needles is to allow for knitting in the round, to make a knitted tube. This is done by casting on the required number of stitches, carefully joining the two ends of the cast-on stitches together, and knitting around and around. When knitting circularly, or "in the round," you are only ever working on the "outside" or the right side of the knitted fabric.

> **Knitting Flat on Circular Needles**—Another very helpful use for circular needles is to knit a large piece of fabric back and forth. This may seem counterintuitive at first, but is in fact very efficient and ergonomic. To knit flat using circular needles, cast on the number of stitches given in your pattern, using one of the needles; ignore the other end, letting it flap around

while you complete your cast-on. Then begin knitting, pretending as if the two needles were not connected. Work across the row, and then turn your work over, just as you would if you were using straight needles. Again pretending the two needles are not connected, begin the next row. As you work, the knitting itself will hang on the connecting "wire," and you should just skooch it along toward the tip of the left-hand needle, just as you would on a straight needle. A great benefit of knitting flat on circular needles is that the weight of the work is centered, rather than hanging off of one side at the end of a straight needle. You will find this provides great relief to your wrists and shoulders. The other major benefit of this method is that you can knit across a very wide piece of fabric, such as the back of an extra-large sweater or the width of a blanket—items that simply will not fit onto the longest of straight needles.

Decreasing: A method for reducing the number of stitches on your needle. Also a technique for manipulating the shape of knitted piece, such making a neck opening rounded or a sleeve smaller at the cuff. The most straightforward and common method of decreasing is to knit (or purl) two stitches together as if they are one. The abbreviation for this action is K2tog (or P2tog). To do this, insert the tip of the right-hand needle into the first two stitches on the left-hand needle, pretending they are one stitch. Then wrap the yarn as usual, and pull one new loop through the two old stitches, letting them both fall off the left-hand needle. Unless otherwise noted, use this method of decreasing for all the projects in this book.

Another method of decreasing is "slip slip knit." The abbreviation for this action is SSK. To do this, slip two stitches, one at a time, from the left hand needle to the right hand needle as if to knit. Then insert the left hand needle into both stitches, behind the right hand needle, and knit the two stitches together. This action is much like K2tog, but you are turning the stitches around on the needle before you knit them together; a K2tog decrease will lean to the right, and an SSK will lean to the left.

Double-Pointed Needles: DPNs are short needles with points on both ends that usually come in sets of four or five. These are used to knit in a circle—or "knitting in the round" (see Circular Needles for more about knitting in the round) when the circumference of your work is too small for a circular needle. In American knitting, knitters typically use four DPNs in their work.

It is much easier to get the hang of DPNs if you introduce them into work that has already been established, such as at the top of a hat. When it is time to change to DPNs, hold the first of your four needles in your right hand, letting it become your working right-hand needle. Insert it into the already established work on your existing left-hand needle at the beginning of a round. Start knitting in the established pattern, and work approximately one-third of the stitches. Then let go of the needle. (The tension of the stitches will keep it in place. It is awkward at first, but don't worry.) Pick up the second of your DPNs and repeat this process, and again with the third. When you have worked all the stitches off your former needle, it will become empty; simply set it aside. Now, insert your fourth needle into the next DPN in the circle, which will be the first one you used. Continue around in this fashion. As you empty your left-hand needle, it will become your right-hand needle, and so on. Continue to use your cast-on tail as a marker to indicate when you have worked all the way around.

Finishing: The assortment of steps and techniques needed to complete a knitting project. Finishing includes things such as blocking, sewing seams, weaving in ends, adding neck finishing and edge treatments, and sewing on buttons. Finishing is usually a love-it or hate-it kind of thing. Many knitters want the sweater or project to be done when the knitting is done, and don't realize the final touches may in some cases take almost as long as the knitting itself. Don't skimp on finishing. You put a lot of time, money, and yourself into your project. Focus your intention on being thorough and proper, and enjoy the details of making your creation as magnificent as it can be. It is good discipline to see the project through to the end with as much purposefulness as you put into it when you started. If you are one of the many knitters who just hate it, consider seeking out an individual who does professional finishing; often one can be found through your local yarn shop. Be prepared to pay a sizable fee for this service, but if you hate it because you find it tedious and time consuming, you will appreciate why they charge as much as they do. If you want to get better at it yourself, and perhaps find the joy in the fine points of the process, see if your local shop or guild offers classes in finishing.

Garter Stitch: The most basic stitch pattern in knitting, garter stitch is created by knitting every row in flat knitting. Both sides look the same. The construction of garter stitch is in fact alternating rows of knit and purl. If you gently pull on the fabric vertically, you can see the row of knit stitches (which look like little Vs) between the ridges of bumpy purl stitch. To create Garter Stitch in the round, you must knit one round, then purl one round.

Gauge: The required number of stitches and rows for a given pattern. You must match the gauge given in the pattern, or else your knitted fabric will not measure to the same dimensions as the pattern, and your project will not be the right size. Nothing is more heartbreaking than completing a project early in your knitting career to find it does not fit or hangs all wrong because you did not take time to properly assess your gauge. Gauge also affects how much yarn will be used.

Before you begin any project, knit a gauge swatch or sample piece. This will enable you to measure the size of your stitches and to practice the stitches used in the project. Most patterns give a gauge in terms of a 4-inch (10 cm) square piece of knitting. Begin using the needle size recommended in your project. This is the *recommended* needle size—a starting point. When you cast on for your swatch, cast on at least 4 stitches more than the number you wish to measure. In other words, if your desired gauge is measured over 20 stitches, cast on 24 or more, and work it for more than 4" in length. This is for several reasons. First, the larger your swatch, the more accurately it can be measured. Second, it is best to measure gauge over a central section of the fabric unobscured by selvage edges, the cast-on, and the needles. If you simply cast on 20 stitches and check to see if it is 4 inches across, you will be doing yourself and your project an injustice.

Use a tape measure, "knit check" tool, or ruler to count the number of stitches you are knitting in the given width (i.e., over 4 inches [10 cm]). If you do not have enough stitches, go to a smaller needle; if you have too many, go to a bigger needle. Keep moving your needle size up or down as needed until you get the stitch count dead on. Remember, it won't take you any longer to knit your project on a smaller needle—if you're getting proper gauge, your stitches are the exact same size as the recommended needle size!

Intarsia: Technique for knitting blocks of color using a strand of each color for each block worked. Rather than having many colors attached to lots of different balls of yarn, each color is often wound onto a bobbin and left to hang off the back of the work until you work your way back to it and need it again. Unlike stranded knitting, such as you would see in a Nordic-style sweater, intarsia blocks are worked without carrying yarns behind the work. Rather, the yarn for each color used is isolated, kept to the confines of its particular color block. When working an intarsia block of color, it is important to twist the two yarns together, "locking" them when you change from one color to the next so as not to knit a slit into your piece. For more information on intarsia and color knitting in general, please consult a well-illustrated knitting reference book.

Joining Work to Knit in the Round: When you join your work into a circle to knit in the round, it is very important to make sure that the stitches are not twisting around the needle. Patterns will say, "Join, being careful not to twist." To see easily whether your stitches are lined up straight, place the needles flat on a table and manipulate the work so that the straight edge of stitches created by your cast-on points in toward the center of the circle. Continuing to use the table as a "third hand" if desired, pick up the needle with the yarn attached to ball coming off it (i.e. the very last stitch you cast-on) in your right hand. Insert the right-hand needle into the first stitch on the left-hand needle and work the first stitch with the yarn that is coming from the right side. This will join the piece into a circle. Then simply begin knitting around and around. Use the cast-on tail as a marker to indicate when you have come all the way around the work and are starting the next round. For a tip on how to better join your work in the round, see The Better Join (page 32).

Picking Up Stitches: This is usually done to create an edge finish or to knit a new part of the project, such as a sleeve, out from a piece of existing fabric. In the patterns in this book, stitches for the sleeves are often picked up at the armhole edge and knit down to the cuff, rather than knitting them separately and sewing them on later. To pick up stitches more neatly and evenly, consider using a crochet hook to help you. With the right side of the fabric facing you, lay down a strand of yarn behind the fabric. Always pick up stitches toward your ball of yarn. Find the location where you will begin picking up stitches, plunge the crochet hook through, and pull through a loop made from the yarn stranding behind. Place this on the right-hand needle. Repeat until you have the number of stitches you need.

To intuitively pick up stitches, note how many stitches you need to pick up. Visually divide this number into 4, and note where these quadrants will be on your piece. For example, when picking up stitches for a sleeve, if you begin at the underarm, the shoulder seam will be halfway. Therefore, halfway to the shoulder seam, you should have a quarter of the stitches already picked up. If you need to make up for extra stitches, place them close to the underarm. Because there are typically more rows to the inch than stitches to the inch, a good rhythm when picking up stitches along a side edge is to pick up into two rows, skip a row, and then repeat. If they don't look right, they are easily pulled out and picked up again. The practice is helpful to hone your skill.

Reading Charts: Knitting charts are a universal visual language for knitting. They are read as if looking at the right side of knitted fabric. When knitting flat, charts are read back and forth, just like the construction of the fabric. Begin in the lower right-hand corner on right-side rows and read from right to left. For wrong-side rows, read from left to right, zigzagging as you go. If knitting in the round, always start at the right-hand side and work right to left, working the symbols exactly as shown.

Although it may feel like learning a new language, becoming comfortable with symbol charts is a wonderful way to become a more intuitive knitter. Once you are familiar with them, the symbols actually look like the completed pattern. This visual language can liberate you from written instructions and long strings of abbreviations such as "P2, K6, P2, C4B, P2, C5F, LT," and other such maddening left-brain fodder. You can begin to interact with the work in such a way that your knitting will actually tell you what to do next. Furthermore, knitting symbols are an international language. Once you are familiar with the basic symbols, you can knit fun and truly exciting projects from any foreign book or magazine that uses them.

Textured and Cable Knitting Charts—Charts represent the right side of the knitted fabric. Therefore, a stitch that should be purled on the wrong side will be shown as a knit stitch. A vertical line or blank square indicates a knit stitch on the right side, a purl stitch on the wrong side, and a horizontal line or dot indicates a purl stitch on the right side, a knit stitch on the wrong side. A symbol key accompanies each knitting chart. If you are working a project with cables, written instructions will accompany the unique symbol for making the cable. A chart for lace will use the symbols specific to the increasing and decreasing methods for lace. You should work the action indicated (i.e., turn the cable or work a decrease as instructed) at the location where the symbol is shown.

Color Knitting Charts—Charts showing patterns for more than one color are read in much the same manner as texture charts, representing the right side of the knitted fabric. A symbol key accompanies the chart, giving you details on which color or symbol used in the chart represents the main color (MC) and the contrast colors (CC). For projects in this book, if multiple contrast color are used, they will be referred to as Contrast Color 1 (CC1), Contrast Color 2 (CC2), and so on. The number of squares shown in a certain color indicates the number of stitches you are to work in that color. Carrying a second color across the back of your knitting to use later is called stranding. Always strand your colors loosely or your tension will be effected. If you strand too tightly, the stitches made with that yarn will recede behind the main color and may disappear entirely.

Reading a Knitting Pattern. Reading a knitting pattern is a lot like following a recipe. All the ingredients you will need are clearly stated at the beginning, and the order in which to add them to the mix is spelled out.

First you will see a statement of the finished size. If the pattern is for a garment with more than one size, pick the size that is the right fit for your recipient. When more than one size is offered, the alternate information is shown in parentheses—for example, "Small (medium, large)." This means that throughout the pattern, the numbers that relate to the size you have chosen will be given in this order. So if you are making a small, you only pay attention to the first set of numbers in front of the parenthesis; if you are making a large, you only read the second set of numbers inside the parentheses.

The next entries are the yarn, the needles, the notions, and the gauge for the project. The materials listing is a straightforward itemization of ingredients. (If you need help finding these items or wish for someone to explain to you what a stitch holder is, for example, please consult your local yarn shop.) Next comes a list of techniques used, with page references directing you to fuller explanations of these techniques in case you need further details about them.

The gauge is a very important component of your project. For an in-depth description of gauge, please refer to the Gauge entry on page 116. The gauge information in the pattern tells you how many stitches and rows you need to achieve in your knitted swatch to make the project come out the intended size. Gauge is typically given in a measurement of 4 square inches, (10 centimeters square in metric). To ensure accuracy when working your gauge swatch, cast on more stitches than the number you actually need to measure. More about this can also be found in the Gauge entry on page 116.

Following the general instructions, the final entries in the pattern may offer variations or optional additions for the project. Just as for a recipe for baking or cooking, it's a good idea to read through the entire pattern before you begin so you can look up anything that is unclear. But don't try too hard to understand everything thoroughly before you begin; some things simply will not be obvious until you have the stitches on the needles.

Note that measurements and needles sizes are given in Imperial/American measurements, followed by metric inside the parentheses. As with the pattern size, here too you should follow the number set that relates to you.

Often a lot of the information in a knitting pattern may appear to be written in some kind of secret code. If an abbreviation is unclear, look it up in the Terms and Abbreviations List (see pages 111–112). If you need further explanation of a technique or term, please consult a good knitting reference book, or ask your knitting mentor for assistance.

Many projects in this book are also accompanied by two wonderful visual tools for understanding the construction and techniques of a project more intuitively: a schematic, and charts or diagrams when relevant. The schematic—the little diagram showing you the overall shape and dimension of the garment or project when is it complete and assembled—can be invaluable in helping you determine what size to make. Charts are given when the instructions include a basic texture or color stitch pattern. For more detailed instructions on reading charts, please consult pages 118–119. Diagrams are given as visual reference and suggestions for embroidered or added touches when an embellishment or a motif is part of the project.

Ribbing: Most familiar as the classic edge treatment traditionally found on sweaters, Ribbing creates a very stretchy, elastic fabric and is generally made up of alternating knit and purl stitches stacked on top of one another. The two most common forms of ribbing are one-by-one ribbing

(1/1 ribbing) and two-by-two ribbing (2/2 ribbing). To knit 1/1 ribbing, knit 1, purl 1 across the row, and for 2/2 ribbing, knit 2, purl 2 across the row. Instruction for knitting these two forms of ribbing are as follows:

Knit One, Purl One Ribbing (worked over an odd number of stitches):
Row 1: (RS) Knit one, * purl one, knit one, repeat from * to end of row.
Row 2: (WS) Purl one, *knit one, purl one, repeat from * to end of row.
Repeat Rows 1 and 2 for desired length or as instructed in your pattern.

Knit Two, Purl Two Ribbing (worked in a multiple of 4 stitches plus 2 extra)
Row 1: (RS) Knit two, * purl two, knit two, repeat from * to end of row.
Row 2: (WS) Purl two, * knit two, purl two, repeat from * to end of row.
Repeat Rows 1 and 2 for desired length or as instructed in your pattern.

When you see an instruction like this for the multiple of stitches needed for a stitch pattern, think of it much like when a cookbook instructs you to use 2 cups of flour plus a tablespoon. In other words, for this stitch pattern (2/2 ribbing), you must first determine what your multiple of 4 is—any number divisible 8, 12, 16, 20, 24, and so on. Then, after you have cast on that number of stitches, add two more at the end, so that the pattern will come out balanced. If it's not making sense, don't think about it too hard; just have faith it will work.

Seed Stitch: A basic and very texturally appealing knit and purl stitch combination. Easy to knit, seed stitch is constructed of a little checkerboard of knit and purl stitches. If you feel bored with basic garter and stockinette stitch projects, seed stitch is a great way to enhance your projects with some interest without increasing the difficulty or adding elements that might be distracting to your focus. Seed stitch is identical on the front and back (right and wrong sides) and is a good pick for any project you want to be reversible. Instructions for seed stitch are as follows:

Seed Stitch (worked over an even number of stitches):
Row 1: (RS) * Knit one, purl one, repeat from * to end of row.
Row 2: (WS) * Purl one, knit one, repeat from * to end of row.
Repeat Rows 1 and 2.

Stockinette Stitch: The stitch most people think of when they think of knitting, stockinette stitch features the smooth, knit stitch on the outside (right side) and the bumpy purl stitch on the inside (wrong side). It is created by stacking rows of the same stitch on top of themselves by alternating rows of knit and purl. This alternation gives stockinette stitch a nice rhythmic quality. Use of a textured or hand-painted/multicolored yarn greatly enhances the basic nature of stockinette stitch. Instructions for working stockinette stitch are as follows:

Stockinette Stitch (worked over any number of stitches).
Row 1: (RS) Knit across the row.
Row 2: (WS) Purl across the row.
Repeat Rows 1 and 2.

Tail (Cast-On Tail) as Marker: The sequence of many simple knit-and-purl stitch patterns depends on attention to the right side (front) and wrong side (back) of the knitted fabric to make the pattern unfold properly. In the first few rows of the pattern instructions, the abbreviations RS (right side) and WS (wrong side) indicate which side will face out. This is always very important, but especially so when a stitch pattern is identical on both the front and back. Tracking rows with a row counter can be very laborious and detracts from the inherent intuitive quality of knitting. For an easy and intuitive way to quickly determine whether the row you are about to knit is a right- or wrong-side row, try this trick, which assumes that Row 1 and all odd rows of your pattern are right-side rows.

Cast on using the Two-Tail or Long Tail Cast-On method (sometimes also called the Double Cast-on). Note that this trick will not work with other methods of casting on. If you are not sure what row you are on, place your knitting down on the table when you are about to begin a row. Point the tip of the left-hand needle toward your right-hand side, just as it will be when you pick it up to knit. Glance down to the cast-on of your work. If the cast-on tail is on the right-hand side of the piece, you are about to begin a right-side row. If the tail is on the left-hand side, you are beginning a wrong-side row.

Three-Needle Bind-Off Technique: A join that produces what looks like a perfect seam and is performed using three needles—two that are holding the live stitches of the pieces to be joined, and a third used for working the bind-off. The basic action is almost identical to that of a standard bind-off. This is a wonderful way to join two pieces of knitting in place of sewing a seam, especially effective when used to join shoulders. The method is also referred to as binding off two pieces together.

To perform this technique, place stitches that may be on hold onto two needles, so that right sides of the fabric face each other and the tips of both needles point in the same direction, If you are joining shoulders, make sure you carefully match left shoulder to left shoulder and right to right. Hold these two needles parallel to each other in your left hand to act as the left-hand needle. Using a third needle as the right-hand needle, insert this right-hand needle through the first stitch on the front needle and the first stitch on the back needle in your left hand. Knit the two stitches together as one and slide them both off their respective needles. Repeat, creating a second stitch on the right-hand needle. Then perform the first bind-off by slipping the first stitch worked over the second stitch worked and off the needle. Repeat the process until all stitches are bound off. Cut the yarn, leaving a 6–10-inch (15–25 cm) tail and draw the tail through the final remaining loop. Weave in the end.

If you are having a hard time visualizing this process, give it a try. If you are still not getting it, please consult a well-illustrated knitting reference book or ask a knitting friend for a demo.

Weaving in the Ends: A crucial part of finishing your work (see Finishing, page 115). Ends, just like knots, have a nasty little tendency to wiggle their way to the front of your work, especially if you have ends front and center—and it seems like there are always ends to weave in at the front and center of a sweater. To minimize the number of ends to weave into your fabric, always try to join a new yarn at the beginning of a row (see Do You Have Enough Left to Knit across the Row? on page 28). To make weaving ends easier, try to leave yarn-end tails that are at least 8 inches (20 cm) long. When weaving in an end on a seam, thread the yarn through a yarn needle and sew up the same path as your seam for about an inch. Then double over the top and trace your path back about an inch. This secures the yarn very well and allows you to cut the yarn flush against the fabric. If you have to weave in an end in the middle of your knitted fabric, work the trajectory of the yarn needle on a diagonal, making sure the yarn you are weaving is not visible from the right side. Then double back and trace your path back to where you started. Again, this allows you to cut the end flush with the fabric. Working on a diagonal minimizes the amount of tug on the end, making it more likely to stay put and not wiggle its way out.

Bobbles: Bobbles are seen on early Aran sweaters as a decorative element. Bobble-like designs are repeatedly seen in early Celtic metal work too. They may be a decorative convention carried over from the Celtic aesthetic.

Celtic Braid: The Braid is a knitted representation of interlacement found carved in Celtic stonework and the early Christian high crosses. This shows an artistic bridge between the traditions, linked by the Aran culture. The knitted braid is also said to be among the skills of early Irish fiber artists, and its unbroken structure is represents the connection between those who have left Ireland in recent centuries and those who stayed behind.

Chevron: This pattern is thought to have arrived in Aran knitting via the Scottish knitting tradition. In the Chevrons one can see references to anchors, wishbones or half-diamonds — all symbols of wealth and fertility. The addition of Irish Moss strengthens these associations. Chevrons are present on early Aran garments, often accompanied by lace-like openwork.

Diamond: These are among the stitches found on the earliest Aran sweaters. Like the Lattice, diamonds are thought to represent the Aran fields surrounded by low stone walls. When filled with Irish Moss stitch, the Diamonds signify fields of man-made soil, created from moss hauled from the beaches over centuries. Diamonds are thought to bring luck.

Hollow Oak: Hollow Oak and its variations are among the oldest stitches found on Aran sweaters. Few direct meanings are attributed to this stitch, but it contains Irish Moss—indicating fertility, bobbles and it echoes the zigzags and diamonds in Celtic stone art that refer to abundance and married life.

Honeycomb: The Honeycomb symbolizes the toil and reward of the hard-working bee. It is a reminder that hard work is rewarded with prosperity.

Horseshoe Cable: The Horseshoe Cable is a variation of the basic Rope Cable. Its makeup is two side-by-side Rope Cables turned on the same row in opposite directions—creating an interesting optical illusion.

Irish Moss: This has come to symbolize the seaweed known as Carrageen Moss. This seaweed is collected from the Aran beaches and hauled up the cliffs to the Islander's small fields where it is mixed with clay and made into workable soil. This practice of literally making arable soil has been practiced for centuries. Irish Moss represents fertility and prosperity.

Lattice: Also know as Trellis or Interlace, Lattice can be seen in Celtic art and jewelry, illuminated manuscripts, and stone crosses. This stitch represents the miles of low stone walls on the Aran Islands that divide and protect the small patches of fertile land. The Lattice is also thought to symbolize the nets used by Aran fishermen.

Moss-Filled Diamond: Moss-Filled Diamonds carry the same significance of the diamond combined with the fertility aspects of Irish Moss. This combination represents the small fields of the Aran Islands filled with man-made soil.

Rope Cable: These simple cables, usually 4 or 6 stitches wide, signify the ropes and nets used by fishermen. Rope Cables are one of the earliest stitches used by Aran knitters. They are thought to bring luck to the wearer.

Tree of Life: This early Aran stitch pattern can often be seen in the welts of early fishing garments. The basic design of the Tree of Life is also found in Celtic stonework. This stitch is a symbol of growth and familial relations. It symbolizes strength of family, and continuation of the family line. It is an overall symbol of unity and is said to bring long life to the wearer.

Trinity Stitch: Also know as Blackberry Stitch. The Trinity Stitch takes its holy name from the manner in which it is made. The pattern is created by "making one from three and three from one," thus evoking the Holy Trinity. It is said the phrase "Father, Son, and Holy Ghost" is repeated over and over by the knitter, much like a Rosary or Mantra.

Zigzag: The basic zigzag shape of this pattern can be seen in Celtic stone and metal work. A single zigzag is thought to represent the jagged cliffs of the Aran Islands. When two or more zigzags appear next to one another they are called Marriage Lines, and are said to symbolize the ups and downs of married life.

Suppliers

Heartfelt thanks are offered to the manufacturers and distributors who have supplied the materials shown in this book. Please contact them to purchase materials or to find a retailer near you.

Blue Sky Alpacas
PO Box 387
St Francis, Minnesota 55070
888-460-8862
www.blueskyalpacas.com
Project: Cloud Pillow

Brown Sheep Co.
100662 County Road 16
Mitchell, Nebraska 69357
800-826-9136
www.brownsheep.com
Project: Heaven and Stars Baby Set

Colinette Yarns
Distributed in the USA by Unique Kolours

The Copper Moth
25 Smith Road
Bedford, New Hampshire 03110
www.coppermoth.com
Natural dyed silk and select fibers in a kaleidoscope of colors created from natural dyes. Colors can range from delicately subtle to brilliantly outrageous. Unusual and often hard to describe, their colors awaken our souls.
Project: Fairy

Cottage Industry
409 South Division Street
Northfield, Minnesota 55057
Unique, certified organic, color-grown cotton and organic Peruvian alpaca.
www.cottageindustry.net
Projects: Travel Accessories, Wrist Warmers

Crystal Palace Yarns

160 23rd Street
Richmond, California 94804
510-237-9988
www.straw.com
Projects: Snowfall Wrap, Sea Aran, Feng Shui Charm, Violets Lavender Sachet, Gifts of Warmth and Compassion Mittens and Scarf, Wisp of Mist Wrist Warmers, Autumn Leaves Blanket

Mission Falls

Distributed in the USA by Unique Kolours

Manos del Uruguay Yarn

PO Box 770
Medford, Massachusetts 02155
781-438-9631 • 888-566-9970
Distributed in the USA by Design Source
Kettle-dyed wool hand dyed by a women's cooperative in Uruguay.
Project: Sky Lake Jacket

Muench Yarns, Inc.

1323 Scott Street
Petaluma, California 94954-1135
800-733-9276
707-763-9477
www.muenchyarns.com
Project: Angel

Mostly Merino

PO Box 878
Putney, Vermont 05346
802-254-7436
merino@together.net
Yarn lovingly produced from a small flock and greenspun in small batches.
Project: Walking Meditation Socks

Moving Mud

http://www.movingmud.com
908.256.6515
4u@movingmud.com
Beautiful handcrafted blown-glass buttons. Moving Mud's extensive list of retail stockists, shows, and exhibits is available on their website. All buttons are unique pieces of art. Please contact Moving Mud for custom requests.
Projects: Heaven and Stars Baby Set, Sea Aran Cardigan, Padma Jacket, Feng Shui Charm

Rowan Yarns

Distributed in the USA by Westminster Fibers
4 Townsend West, Unit 8
Nashua, New Hampshire 03063
603-886-5041
wfibers@aol.com • www.knitrowan.com
Project: Fairy

Unique Kolours
Distributors of Colinette and Mission Falls
28 North Bacton Hill Road
Malvern, Pennsylvania 19355

1-800-242-2DYEFOR
www.uniquekolours.com
Projects: Padma Jacket, Black Sand Vest

bibliography and further reading

Berliner, Helen. *Enlightened by Design.* Boston: Shambhala Publications, 1999.

Cameron, Julia. *Walking in this World.* New York: Tarcher, 2003.

Chodron, Pema. *The Wisdom of No Escape and the Path of Loving Kindness.* Boston: Shambhala Publications, 1991.

Editors of Vogue Knitting. *Vogue Knitting: the Ultimate Knitting Book.* New York: Sixth and Spring Books, 2002.

Emerson, Jayne and Margaret Docherty. *Simply Felt: 20 Easy and Elegant Designs in Wool.* Loveland, CO: Interweave Press, 2004.

England, Allison. *Aromatherapy and Massage for Mother and Baby.* Rochester, Vermont: Healing Arts Press, 2000.

Manning, Tara Jon. "Aran Hand Knitting—History, Design and Technique." Master's thesis, Colorado State University, 1997.

———. Celtic Images and Family Patterns: Folklore of the Aran Sweater. Interweave Knits, Fall 1997, pg 48.

———. *Mindful Knitting: Inviting Contemplative Practice to the Craft.* Rutland, VT: Tuttle Publications, 2004.

Marshall, John. *Make Your Own Japanese Clothes: Patterns and Ideas for Modern Wear.* Kodansha America, 1998.

Reincken, Sunnhild. *Making Dolls.* Edinburgh: Floris Books, 2003.

Sealey, Maricristin. *Kinder Dolls: A Waldorf Doll-Making Handbook.* Gloucestershire: Hawthorn Press, 2001.

Shurety, Sarah. *Feng Shui for Your Home: An Illustrated Guide to Creating a Harmonious, Happy and Prosperous Living Environment.* London: Rider & Co., 1997.

Starmore, Alice. *Aran Knitting.* Loveland, CO: Interweave Press, 1997.

Vickrey, Anne. *The Art of Feltmaking: Basic Techniques for Making Jewelry, Miniatures, Dolls, Buttons, Wearables, Puppets, Masks and Fine Art Pieces.* New York: Watson-Guptill Publications, 1997.

———. *Needle Felting: Art Techniques and Projects.* Geneva, NY: Craft Works Publishing, 2002.

Wilson, Roberta. *Aromatherapy: Esssential Oils for Vibrant Health and Beauty.* New York, Avery: 2002.

Trungpa, Chogyam. *Shambhala: Sacred Path of the Warrior.* Boston: Shambhala Publications, 1988.

———. *Great Eastern Sun: The Wisdom of Shambhala.* Boston: Shambhala Publications, 2001.

local yarn shops

Keep the local knitting community in your area flourishing by supporting your local yarn and crafts shops. These retailers are often the heart and hub of knitting groups, friendships, and support networks. To find a local yarn store in your area, run a search through your favorite internet search engine for "your town" + "yarn shop." Yarn shops come and go, so check your current phone book for up-to-date contact information.

finding or founding a knitting group in your area

Ask at your local yarn shop for local knitting group and guild information. Consider starting a group in your area by posting a notice at a community center, yarn shop, church, or coffeehouse. Many already established groups and guilds can be located through a simple web search engine search using the key words "knitting group + your town." Also check with The Knitting Guild Association (www.tkga.com) to see if a formal guild exists near you.

mindful knitting workshops and retreats

Join Tara, her special guests, and other curious, remarkable, and fun knitters at a Mindful Knitting Workshop or Retreat. Participate in Mindful Knitting and Mindfulness Meditation instruction, and make lasting friendships. Explore the themes of generosity, compassion, and basic goodness while engaging with the natural environment. Have fun while you pamper yourself and knit the weekend away! For details, locations, and schedules, please visit www.mindful knitting.com.

start a mindful knitting group in your hometown

If you have found the Mindful Knitting approach to knitting as a contemplative practice helpful, consider forming a Mindful Knitting group in your area. In establishing this kind of community or *sangha*, you will be able to share and explore your own views about how knitting is fulfilling and both find and provide support for other likeminded knitters. You could simply meet as a social group with similar interests, or take a more formal approach by using the themes and instructions in this book to further explore using your cherished handwork as a forum for working with your world mindfully. Gather a few friends or post a notice at your place of worship, meditation center, local yarn shop, or favorite coffee shop. Consider discussing how your knitting sangha can share its inspiration and compassion—perhaps by teaching others to knit or by forming a charity knitting project. Remember, your ability to inspire and share the elements of basic goodness and compassion is limited only by you.

shambhala training international

Shambhala Training is the secular study and practice of Shambhala warriorship—the tradition of compassion, human bravery, and leadership. The Shambhala warrior's path shows us how to address the challenges of daily life and the modern world as opportunities for contemplative practice and social action. In a series of weekend meditation workshops for both beginning and experienced meditators, Shambhala Training uses a simple and profound technique of mindfulness meditation that cultivates mindfulness, compassion, and awareness. By looking directly at our own experiences utilizing such a mindfulness meditation technique, we are able to connect with the basic dignity that exists in all beings. More information about Shambhala Training can be found at www.shambhala.org.

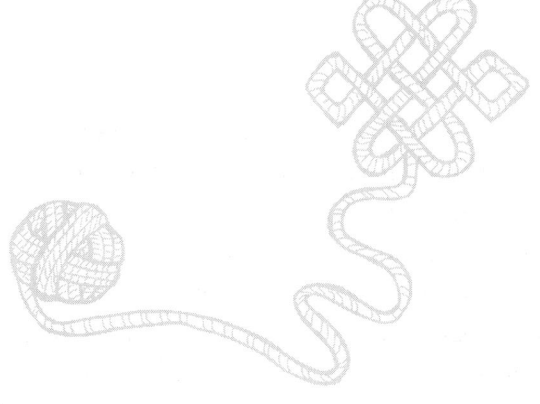